AD Non Fiction
248 G3

Gerelds,   s
fall forwa   1
"The Co

D0615591

ALWAYS
FALL FORWARD

Life lessons I'll never forget from "The Coach"

TODD GERELDS
AUTHOR OF WOODLAWN

*The nonfiction imprint of
Tyndale House Publishers, Inc.*

Visit Tyndale online at www.tyndale.com.

Visit Tyndale Momentum online at www.tyndalemomentum.com.

Visit Todd Gerelds online at www.toddgerelds.com.

TYNDALE, *Tyndale Momentum*, and Tyndale's quill logo are registered trademarks of Tyndale House Publishers, Inc. The Tyndale Momentum logo is a trademark of Tyndale House Publishers, Inc. Tyndale Momentum is the nonfiction imprint of Tyndale House Publishers, Inc., Carol Stream, Illinois.

Always Fall Forward: Life Lessons I'll Never Forget from "The Coach"

Copyright © 2018 by Thomas Todd Gerelds. All rights reserved.

Cover photograph of stadium copyright © Dmytro Aksonov/Getty Images. All rights reserved.

Cover photograph of leather texture copyright © RedDaxLuma/Deposit Photos. All rights reserved.

Interior photographs copyright © Todd Kwarcinski/TKphotography. All rights reserved, and used with permission.

Author photograph by Jennifer Gerelds, copyright © 2015. All rights reserved.

Designed by Ron C. Kaufmann

Edited by Sarah Rubio

Published in association with the literary agency WTA Services, LLC, Franklin, TN.

Unless otherwise indicated, all Scripture quotations are taken from the *Holy Bible*, New Living Translation, copyright © 1996, 2004, 2015 by Tyndale House Foundation. Used by permission of Tyndale House Publishers, Inc., Carol Stream, Illinois 60188. All rights reserved.

Scripture quotations marked MSG are taken from *THE MESSAGE*, copyright © 1993, 1994, 1995, 1996, 2000, 2001, 2002 by Eugene H. Peterson. Used by permission of NavPress. All rights reserved. Represented by Tyndale House Publishers, Inc.

Scripture quotations marked NIrV are taken from the Holy Bible, *New International Reader's Version,*® *NIrV.*® Copyright © 1995, 1996, 1998, 2014 by Biblica, Inc.® Used by permission. All rights reserved worldwide.

Scripture quotations marked NIV are taken from the Holy Bible, *New International Version,*® *NIV.*® Copyright © 1973, 1978, 1984, 2011 by Biblica, Inc.® Used by permission. All rights reserved worldwide.

For information about special discounts for bulk purchases, please contact Tyndale House Publishers at csresponse@tyndale.com, or call 1-800-323-9400.

ISBN 978-1-4964-2480-8

Printed in the United States of America

24	23	22	21	20	19	18
7	6	5	4	3	2	1

9001140577

*To two men God used to save my dad's life—
Wales Goebel, for sharing the truth of the
gospel, the power of God for salvation.
Julius Clark, for loving my dad, being a friend
to him, and loving his neighbor when it wasn't
necessarily the popular thing to do.*

CONTENTS

Football is a great game, but it's a lousy god. I grew up the son of a coach, just like Todd Gerelds, and like him I had to learn this valuable lesson. It's true that anything we love more, serve more, fear more, or value more than God Almighty is an idol. However, this game can really teach us some life lessons that are of great value.

I have always considered football to be the greatest sport ever invented, because it teaches lessons that other sports just don't teach. Like many of you who are reading this devotional, I often go back to the lessons I learned from not only playing football but also having football as the family business throughout my childhood and young adult life. I love this devotional that Todd has put together because it uses football to teach biblical and life truths that are much more important than the sport itself. God has really pressed upon me a passion to see men come to know Christ and impact their families, their churches, and their society by truly understanding why God made them men in the first place. This devotional can be a great resource for men to be discipled and then be equipped to disciple other men.

Many men have been told over and over that they need to be the spiritual leaders of their homes but have no idea what that looks like in their daily lives. This devotional takes the cue from Jesus Himself by using parables that relate to football terminology to drive home a much bigger and more important biblical truth.

Do you have to play football to be a real man? Of course not—some of the most devout followers of Christ I have ever known have never played football—but you can still learn many great principles from the sport. The bottom line is that true biblical masculinity is found in the example of the "new Adam," Jesus Christ. So I encourage you to consume this devotional with one goal in mind: to become a disciple of Christ who advances the kingdom of God. I don't know of any man who would go onto the gridiron and never desire to be put in the game. You have been in the stands long enough—time to get on the field of battle.

Rick Burgess
Cohost of The Rick and Bubba Show; *coauthor of*
How to Be a Man: Pursuing Christ-Centered Masculinity

INTRODUCTION

My dad, Tandy Gerelds, was a football coach. He began his coaching career at Woodlawn High School in 1965. He actually graduated from Woodlawn just four years prior to coming on staff as an assistant coach. During those four years, he attended Auburn University, where he walked on and became a leader for the 1963 Southeastern Conference Championship baseball team. Dad was an assistant football coach at Woodlawn until 1971, when then–head coach Bill Burgess decided to take a job as head coach at Oxford High School in Northeast Alabama. So in 1971, Dad became the head football coach at one of the largest, most prestigious schools in the state of Alabama. He was twenty-nine years old and doing what he loved.

Dad's first year as head coach coincided with the federal government's decision to begin busing African American students from all-black high schools to predominantly white high schools in inner-city Birmingham, Alabama.

To truly understand what a chaotic, yet significant, time this was, one would need to have a better understanding of the years preceding this decision.

Every bad thing you've ever heard or seen regarding the South, and Alabama in particular, was on full display in the decade before Dad became head coach at Woodlawn High School—police dogs, fire hoses, bombings, Martin Luther King Jr. being put in a Birmingham jail cell. Black kids had no reason to believe that anything good could come from being forced to go to school with white kids. Everything they had ever seen regarding "white folks" came from television. And none of it was good.

After a rough two years, in August of 1973, Dad decided to have his first "camp." This was his term for his team practicing two to three times a day and eating and sleeping in the Woodlawn gym. He thought that having the team all eat, sleep, practice, and literally *live* together might bring about some much-needed team unity. It was at this time that an evangelist named Wales Goebel requested permission to share the gospel with the football team. Dad initially declined his request. At the time, Dad believed that faith in Christ would make you soft. He was sure that if his players placed their faith in Jesus, they wouldn't be tough enough to be good football players. Dad's conversion was well documented in my book *Woodlawn* and the subsequent movie by the same name. The Woodlawn story details how a cynical young coach was overwhelmed by the supernatural love that transformed his football team. He came to recognize that his earlier assumptions about toughness were completely incorrect.

My dad began to realize that putting others before self was the true mark of a man. He also knew that no one did that perfectly except Jesus Christ. God's Word teaches us that "there is no greater love than to lay down one's life for one's friends" (John 15:13). And that rather than making us weak, God's Spirit does the opposite: "God gave us his Spirit. And the Spirit doesn't make us weak and fearful. Instead, the Spirit gives us power and love. He helps us control ourselves" (2 Timothy 1:7, NIrv).

One day while Dad and I were talking about Jesus, Dad said, "I'll bet Jesus would have been a great football player." I smiled and agreed. I wondered aloud, "What position?" Dad, without hesitation, replied, "Free safety." A free safety is sometimes called the quarterback of the defense. He generally calls the coverages in the secondary. Great free safeties are known for being smart and tough and are usually big hitters. Dad went on to explain that Scripture teaches that Jesus was a carpenter and the son of a carpenter (see Mark 6:3). He had worked hard physically from the time he was a kid. His response to adversity throughout His life showed a remarkable character and grit. He would be fearless, tough, and dependable. He was strong (see Luke 2:40).

God has made it clear that being a man goes far beyond muscles and testosterone. "Physical training is good, but training for godliness is much better, promising benefits in this life and in the life to come" (1 Timothy 4:8). Manhood's best example is Jesus Christ. He was a man's man. He was the fiercest lover of people who ever lived. He *always* loved. He gave Himself up for His bride, the church. And I'll bet He'd have been a great free safety.

Over the following pages, I'll share with you things my dad said in his unique way as he coached his players and trained me to become a man. My goal is to communicate in a way that will engage you as a real man. I believe all aspects of our manhood are meant to be addressed as we grow in our relationship with our Father (see Luke 10:27). I will incorporate Scripture so that the truths Dad taught will be combined with God's Word to give you a meaningful, thoughtful, and powerful Bible-based theme you can take into each week.

PART 1

"Whatever work we are called to

can be a means for us to honor God."

See What You Hit

I run with purpose in every step.

I am not just shadowboxing.

1 CORINTHIANS 9:26

It felt like a lightning bolt had run from the base of my skull, through my neck and shoulders, and down my right arm. The pain was excruciating. I'd just received my first "stinger," or "burner," an intensely painful nerve injury. It was football spring training during my sophomore year of high school. I had taken on a senior fullback named Chris Haynes in a drill known as the Oklahoma. Normally, the Oklahoma drill pits three offensive linemen against three defensive linemen. A coach tells the running back behind the offensive line where to run. The same coach lets the offensive linemen know where to block the defenders. There is also a wide receiver positioned to take on a defensive back several yards behind the defensive line. We were running a scaled-down version of the Oklahoma where it was one on one between an offensive and defensive lineman with a defensive back—me—positioned about five or six yards off the line of scrimmage. My job was to see which way the running back cut from the line of scrimmage and to stop him. Chris's job was to get past me. There was no question who won our encounter. As Chris cut to his left, my right, I came flying up to meet him, head down. He planted me on my back as he continued on to score.

After my stinger, Dad taught me that I need to be looking at the ballcarrier when I tackle him. "See what you're hitting!" he would bark.

In recent years, more and more emphasis has been put on player safety in an effort to avoid catastrophic injuries in football. Dad's coaching was ahead of his time in this regard. Back when Dad coached, it was common to hear, "Put your head down and go!" Somehow, Dad knew this wasn't the best way. Seeing who you are tackling might mean that you don't deliver as devastating a blow as you want, but it also means that you are far less likely to miss the tackle. As an incredibly important bonus, injury is *far* less likely when your head is up.

God designed us with a yearning to have an impact. We want to make a difference. In our day-to-day lives, this desire for impact needs to be controlled by the Holy Spirit to ensure we have the kind of impact God intends. Scripture teaches us that discipline, self-control, and keeping our eyes on our target (not running aimlessly) help us to avoid missing the mark. When I was managing sales reps for a large pharmaceutical company, I used to tell the reps, "Don't mistake activity for achievement." Oftentimes in the work world we allow ourselves to get very busy with activities that seem necessary but are not actually moving us toward our objectives. Whatever our jobs, seeing what we hit means establishing clear objectives and then aligning our actions with them.

In the Scripture passage from which today's verse is taken, Paul compares his spiritual life to athletic training. He says that he doesn't act without clear purpose in mind.

We need to be like Paul and know what we are trying to hit spiritually. Putting our heads down and plowing through is our natural instinct, but we may miss God's objective when we do that. Let's ask God to give us discipline and self-control. Let us be imitators of the examples of godly character God has given us in Scripture and in the people around us.

I challenge you to read the Gospels to see Jesus' perfect character. I suggest reading a chapter of the Gospels every day until you've read through all of them. Once you've finished them all, you can start again. That's what I do. It keeps the heart and character of Jesus right in front of me. I also encourage you to seek the counsel of a godly mentor in your church. Know what you are aiming for and keep your eyes on your target. You are far more likely to hit it. And you are far less likely to give yourself a spiritual stinger or injure others in your efforts.

TO GO DEEPER THIS WEEK . . .
» Read 1 Corinthians 9:25-27.
» Read Philippians 3:17.

1. What are some situations in which you might be tempted to plow forward without seeing what you hit?
2. Who are some possible mentors you could seek out for counsel in your life?

Outwork Your Opponent

Work willingly at whatever you do, as though you were
working for the Lord rather than for people.

COLOSSIANS 3:23

As my junior year of high school approached, my friends and I spent the summer in the weight room and on the football field, preparing for summer practice. When the day came for practice to start, we boarded buses in Tuscumbia, Alabama, and set out for the remote, rural town of Cullman, Alabama. The destination? St. Bernard Abbey. That's right—a monastery located almost smack-dab in the middle of the state. We would spend the next week practicing twice a day in the August heat. At night, we would retire to our unair-conditioned dorm rooms. Dad wanted us to develop an unrivaled work ethic.

The demands Dad placed on his team were met with varying degrees of acceptance. Some players were eager to please the new coach, doing whatever they could to catch his eye. Some were going to do their best regardless. It was just the way they were wired. Others were more skeptical. I think they may have wondered if the ends justified the means, so to speak. Some probably didn't think they needed the extreme level of conditioning required by this new coach. For me, it was a little easier. I knew this coach. I knew his track record. I knew that he knew what worked and that his plans were for *our* good.

Since I was a little boy, I had heard my dad emphasize the importance of *hard work*. He felt that this was the one variable that his team had a say in when a game was on the line. Out in the isolated heat of Cullman, Alabama, Dad explained to us that hard work might actually allow us to beat a more talented opponent.

If you have thirty-five players and your opponent has a hundred, there's nothing you can do about that. If your opponent's offensive line averages six feet four inches and 285 pounds and your defensive line averages six feet and 210 pounds, you can't change that either. Those are objective variables that you live with. What you can change is how hard you are willing to work for your goal. If you have trained yourself to work harder than your opponent, you may be in a better position to win. Dad's motivation for the legendary conditioning of his teams was not punitive. It was so that fatigue would not hinder his teams from accomplishing their goals.

More than halfway through that first season, our hard

work finally paid off. First, we fought from behind on the road against a rival team, Brooks, to win a 20–14 victory. Two weeks later, our scrappy, 2–5 team faced off against 7–1 Lauderdale County. They definitely appeared bigger and stronger. Nonetheless, when the final horn sounded, somehow we had eked out a 9–7 win. Hard work had prevailed!

Since graduating from college and moving out into the real world, I have found that Dad's philosophy of hard work applies equally in business. Work ethic often separates people of similar aptitude in the workforce. I have worked with people who were enormously talented but lacked a strong work ethic. They never lived up to their potential. On the flip side, I've worked with people who weren't as gifted but got everything they could out of their ability. I believe a team has a better chance at success with the latter type of person.

Our motivation for work should be to honor our Lord in everything we do so that we can accomplish those things for which He designed us. In New Testament times, people who owed a debt could sell themselves to the lender for the purpose of paying off their debt. The term for this position has been translated as "bond servant," "bond slave," or simply, "servant" or "slave." The one to whom they'd sold themselves would be their master. Today Paul's words would equally apply to anyone who has a boss who oversees his or her work.

In Colossians 3:23-24 Paul tells these servants to

give all they've got in obedience to their earthly masters, knowing that they are really working for their true Master, Jesus. He reminds them that their real payday is the eternal reward they will receive from Him.

Paul makes no distinction in what *type* of work we do. Whatever work we are called to can be a means for us to honor God. Our work shouldn't be good only when others are watching or done to win praise from other people. But instead, our motivation should be to glorify Christ because He is our *true* boss. As we do this, it is essential that we keep in mind that Christ's work on the cross is sufficient for our salvation. Our work "for the Lord rather than for people" should be freeing, as we are no longer bound by the opinions and expectations of people, but instead are able to joyously work from a heart of gratitude. Today let us approach our work with a grateful heart, seeking to bring honor to our Father as we excellently labor in whatever work He has called us to do.

TO GO DEEPER THIS WEEK . . .
» Read Colossians 3:22-24.

1. In your daily activities, what are some things you can do to remind yourself who you're actually working for?
2. Can you think of times in your own life where you have seen hard work overcome obstacles?

Couch Sessions

We will speak the truth in love, growing in every way
more and more like Christ.

EPHESIANS 4:15

Aconcerned father was sitting on the couch in the head football coach's office. My dad was sitting at his desk, listening. The man's son was a backup on Dad's state championship defense. Most of his playing time had been relegated to late in games when the outcome had already been decided. The player's dad loved his son and wanted to see him succeed. He pointed out that his son had made several interceptions in his limited playing time. "Coach, I'm just wondering why my son isn't playing more." Coach paused, then explained to the concerned father that, indeed, his son had made plays late in games when teams were launching Hail Mary passes. "But," he explained, "football is a violent game. When the game is on the line and things get really physical, we're not confident that he is hard nosed enough to come sprinting up to where bodies are flying around." With just a few words, Dad had given insight from his broader perspective that included hours of practice time. I'm quite sure that this conversation was eye opening for this father. It most assuredly helped him better deal with the real issues.

As believers we are called to "speak the truth in love." When the parents of Dad's players were unable to do this with their sons, Dad had to hold what he called couch sessions. During these sessions, caring yet often disgruntled parents would come into his office to voice their concerns. Dad would always listen. He loved the kids who played for him. But he also knew that allowing them to believe things that weren't true wasn't helpful for them. In fact, it would hurt them in the end.

My dad also loved me and my two sisters. And from the day he came to know Jesus, he made sure to tell us every day that he loved us. He also made sure to teach us things that frankly, as young people, we didn't always want to hear. Dad was committed to helping us become the adults God intended us to be, and he wasn't seeking to win a popularity contest with me or my sisters. Dad knew that God loved him. That was enough for him. Winning the approval of other people, even his children, wasn't as important.

As a father, I have found that, in dealing with my four daughters, there are times when it would be much easier to let things slide. There are definitely times when I know that I'm going to have to be the bad guy, by speaking the truth in love.

One such situation concerned a relationship one of my daughters had developed with a young man. The relationship seemed fine at first, but over time my wife and I began to notice behaviors from the young man that really concerned us. As I began to talk to my daughter about it, she *definitely* thought of me as the bad guy. Still, she needed to hear the truth. At various times over several weeks, I vacillated between speaking the truth in love and totally blowing it as my temper and pride got the best of me. Ultimately, God worked out the situation—sometimes by using me and my wife, and sometimes by lovingly working *despite* us.

In Ephesians 4:15-16 Paul describes the results of speaking the truth in love. Paul calls the church the body of Christ. He teaches us that speaking the truth in love allows this body to grow and work properly. This means that when I lose my cool, or avoid conflict, I may be depriving someone of the encouragement, correction, or instruction God intends them to receive through me.

The critical factor in these conversations is *love*. Love has the other person in mind. Love allows truth to have its intended impact. As we live, work, and love this week, we will inevitably have opportunities to be used by God to reveal truth to those around us. As these opportunities arise, let us ask God for the ability to put the other person's interests above our own. Let us look for opportunities to encourage and facilitate growth. Despite the discomfort these kinds of conversations may sometimes cause, God tells us that as we "couch" them in His amazing love, they will be used to help His children "grow up in every way" (Ephesians 4:15, ESV)—into Christ.

TO GO DEEPER THIS WEEK...
» Read Ephesians 4:15-16.

1. Can you think of a situation in your life in which someone spoke the truth in love to you? How did you respond? What was the impact?
2. Are there any "couch sessions" you need to have with anyone in your life at this time?

Your Stance Is Critical

Anyone who listens to my teaching and follows it is wise,
like a person who builds a house on solid rock.
Though the rain comes in torrents and the floodwaters
rise and the winds beat against that house,
it won't collapse because it is built on bedrock.

MATTHEW 7:24-25

"Get your rump down! Head up! Back flat!" Dad slowly walked around me as I squatted down between his recliner and the television, my right hand resting on the floor in front of me, directly beneath my forehead. He pushed me forward and back to make sure that my weight was equally positioned on my feet and hand. When too much weight was on my hand, his push to my rear caused me to fall onto my face. His nudges to my forehead sent me sprawling onto my backside when my weight was too heavy on my feet. Dad understood the importance of a firm foundation.

As I continued to play football over the years, I saw that good coaches emphasized the importance of proper stance regardless of the position I played. Backs, ends, and linemen all need to be able to explode into action when the ball is snapped. If their stance, or foundation, is out of balance, the players won't be properly prepared to react or respond when they are called upon to execute their responsibilities. Even after a play starts, if a player is engaged in the action, his body should maintain this proper foundation. The results of trying to engage an opponent with a faulty foundation can be painful.

When I was a senior, our team was preparing to play Bradshaw High School. My dad made sure to brief me about one of their defensive tackles. On certain plays, the fullback (me) would "fill" for the pulling guard. This basically meant that whoever was in front of the offensive guard would be left unblocked as the guard led the tailback around the end. It was the fullback's job to fill that gap and block the man who would be charging through the space left by the pulling guard. Dad explained that this defensive tackle was big and strong. But he was a sophomore. I thought, *I'll be able to handle this guy.* The time came for me to fill for our guard. The young defensive tackle (who later became a major college defensive lineman) met me in the gap. His foundation was solid, and despite his six-foot-three stature, he was able to stay low to the ground. I thought I'd be able to get into his body and drive him out of the play . . . until the back of my head hit the turf. He plowed me. All of our power comes from a solid foundation.

Over the course of my career as a salesperson, sales trainer, and sales manager, I've seen that the foundation for success has been communication. Genuine communication with customers, peers, trainees, or the people I have led has been essential to the attainment of our objectives. In the corporate world, factors beyond our control may adversely affect the environment in which we operate. In these situations, the lack of foundational, clear, honest, and mutually constructive communication often leads to figuratively being knocked on our backsides.

Jesus taught His disciples a similar lesson about foundations in Matthew 7:24-27. He told His disciples that those who listen to Him and do what He says are like builders who build on firm foundations. He said that even if storms with winds and floods come along, homes built on these kinds of foundations will stand. On the other hand, those who don't listen and obey Him are like builders who lay bad foundations. If the same storm hits these homes, they will be totally lost.

Jesus' point is that the integrity of the entire structure is dependent on its foundation. It's important to note that Jesus said that a good foundation is based on *obedience* to Him, not just intellectual agreement with Him. Scripture tells us that we are saved by grace through faith in Christ (see Ephesians 2:8). By implication, Jesus is saying that true faith is demonstrated as we obey Him (see James 1:21-27 and 1 John 2:3-11). His Word tells us that

He has prepared good works for us to do before we even do them (see Ephesians 2:10). Today, let us ask our Father to give us eyes to see Him at work in the world around us and to give us grace to build a firm foundation by acting on our faith.

TO GO DEEPER THIS WEEK . . .
» Read Matthew 7:24-27.
» Read Ephesians 2:8-10.
» Read James 1:21-27.
» Read 1 John 2:3-11.

1. Can you think of situations you have witnessed where it became apparent that foundation issues were causing big problems? What happened? Were they resolved? If so, how? If not, how could they have been repaired?
2. Are there any areas where your "stance" may be out of balance? Ask God to empower you in any situations where you are having a difficult time obeying Him. Or, ask God to show you any areas that may be blind spots where you are unaware of disobedience.

Always Fall Forward

Forgetting the past and looking forward to what lies ahead,
I press on to reach the end of the race and receive the heavenly
prize for which God, through Christ Jesus, is calling us.

PHILIPPIANS 3:13-14

Most football fans have heard the saying, "It's a game of inches." Truly, less than an inch may be the difference between winning and losing a football game. Keeping that in mind, my dad coached me and other backs and ball carriers to "always fall forward." His point was to get every possible inch out of every play. This means that if you rip off a nine-yard run on first down and are hit a yard short of the marker, you should do everything you can to fall forward and extend the ball for the first down. However, there are times when the marker or goal line may be completely unattainable. The running back may be hit three yards deep in the backfield. But Dad coached us even in those circumstances—*especially* in those circumstances—to always fall forward. Falling forward to make it second and eleven instead of second and thirteen may be the difference in the game. Often, the extra inches may seem insignificant at the time. It may even seem senseless for the running back to strain forward to get an extra yard when the actual goal seems so far out of reach. But you never know what the next play will bring, and every inch counts.

In 2 Corinthians 11:24-27, Paul speaks of various times when it seemed that the enemy was winning. He was beaten with rods three times; five times he received the forty lashes minus one; he was shipwrecked, stoned, and so on. You have to think there were times when Paul wondered what benefit there was for him to continue to fight through these apparent defeats. Yet each time he continued to strain forward. Paul emphasizes this in today's verses.

Today, you will inevitably face battles. Some may be against people who are intentionally aiming to prevent you from living out your purpose. Some battles may be against your own human nature, which is seeking to overpower the Spirit who indwells you. In my years as a salesperson I have had innumerable days on which I have driven hours to a company only to be turned away by the receptionist because my customer "isn't seeing reps today." Frustrated but undaunted, I walk back to my car and head off to the next customer on the list. I arrive and happily greet the receptionist, who tells me, "Oh, I'm so sorry. She's out of town this week." Sigh. Back in the car, I map out the route to the next business. I arrive after a fifteen-minute drive and the customer quickly lets me know that he doesn't have time to talk and that until we can do something about the price of our product, he won't be able to use it. Sitting in my car, understandably frustrated, I have a choice—will I keep fighting on for that "extra yard"? Am I going to try to get everything out of the day that I possibly can, or am I just going to give up?

The Bible teaches us that our *old nature* battles against the *new creation* we have become through faith in Jesus (see Ephesians 4:22; Colossians 3:9; Romans 6:6; 2 Corinthians 5:17). There have been times in my life when I have forgotten this truth. *I've blown it! No point fighting anymore.* It's kind of an all-or-nothing mentality. In Romans 7:14-25, the apostle Paul reveals that he has these same types of thoughts at times. He concludes the passage with this truth: "The answer is in Jesus Christ our Lord."

As Christians we have the Holy Spirit living in us. I don't *ever* have to give up, and neither do you. Pray to your Father that today you will trust that He goes before you and that He will win these battles for and through you. Ask Him to help you to forget what lies behind (past failures, sins, or habits) and to enable you to press on to be the person He has made you to be. You and I can do this with the knowledge that Jesus has already won the game.

At times we may *feel* doomed to failure. That is a lie. There is no failure, as Christ has already won. When you recognize that you've missed the mark, make sure that you *fall forward*. Repent and move on. Your victory is secure.

TO GO DEEPER THIS WEEK...

» Read Romans 6:6; 2 Corinthians 5:17;
  Ephesians 4:22; and Colossians 3:9.
» Read Romans 7:14-25.
» Read 2 Corinthians 11:24-27.
» Read Ephesians 6:10-13.

1. Has there ever been a situation where you felt you had blown it and considered giving up? What did you do? Did you decide to fight on? What was the outcome?
2. Can you think of a time when a seeming failure led you to a deeper dependence on God, or when you gained some new insight or knowledge? Write out your experience.

Scrape!

When troubles of any kind come your way, consider it an
opportunity for great joy. For you know that when your
faith is tested, your endurance has a chance to grow.

JAMES 1:2-3

For the first several years I played football, I played defensive back. Rarely did I get tangled up in the area known as "the box"—an area which extended two to three yards on each side of the line of scrimmage. But heading into my junior year of high school, I had grown a bit, so the coaches decided to try me as a middle linebacker. Dad taught me and the other middle linebackers to pursue the ballcarrier from the inside out. If the play was moving away from us, we were not to try to get ahead of our opponent, allowing him to cut back. Instead, we were to pursue the runner moving upfield, maintaining an inside position relative to him. This inside-out pursuit often requires the linebacker to take on blockers as he moves upfield in pursuit of the runner. This act of moving through the blockers is called "scraping." Sometimes a linebacker will instinctively take off parallel to the running back, straight toward the sideline—what commentators refer to as overpursuit. This instinct is driven by the desire to make the play while avoiding the difficulties of taking on a blocker. If you overpursued on my dad's team, you would hear him yelling, "Scrape! Scrape!"

On November 2, 1984, I had my best night ever as a running back. Against our biggest rival, Sheffield High School, I carried the ball nineteen times and rushed for 160 yards and four touchdowns. A huge number of the yards I gained that night were due to the Sheffield linebackers taking off to their left or right instead of scraping. Several times during the game, on what we called the Belly play, the linebackers overpursued, running toward the sideline, and I cut right back behind them for big gains. I believe both of those linebackers were better athletes than I was. They were both really quick and were good tacklers. Still, in this situation, their speed and athleticism took them out of the play. Scraping and engaging the mess in front of them would have prevented my long gains.

I know that there have been many times when my primary goal was to take the fastest, easiest path out of a difficult situation. But I have learned that sometimes God intends for us to go through troubles, as He uses them for His good purposes and for our good. James 1:2-4 tells us to be joyful as we go through difficult times, knowing that God is using these circumstances to bring us to maturity in Him.

In looking at the life of Paul, we can't help but notice

that the path he took in his quest to reach those who didn't know Jesus led him through some extraordinarily difficult circumstances. In 2 Corinthians 11:23-27 he elaborates on the seemingly impossible number of obstacles that he navigated on his life's journey. One of these episodes is recorded in Acts 16:22-32. Paul and his friend Silas were arrested and severely beaten with wooden rods. They were then thrown into the innermost part of the jail and even had their feet clamped down in stocks.

Instead of trying to escape, Paul and Silas started singing and praying. They were keenly aware that Jesus was *with them* in their trouble. Even when a miracle occurred and their chains fell off and all the prison doors opened, Paul and Silas didn't leave. Instead, they shared God's truth about salvation through Jesus with their jailer.

This week, let's ask our Father to give us the wisdom to understand that our path to knowing and serving Him may require us to "scrape." Let's ask Him not for an easier path but for His grace to sustain us through the trials that will come. Let's ask Him to let us find Him in these situations and to help us trust that He will be with us through whatever we face.

TO GO DEEPER THIS WEEK . . .

» Read Isaiah 55:9.
» Read Acts 16:22-26.
» Read 2 Corinthians 11:23-27.

1. Reflect on a time when it seemed you were having to go through trials to get where you thought God was leading you. What were your thoughts at the time? Was God closing a door? Did you want to go around the problem?
2. Why do you think we see this pattern of God not only allowing but also sometimes leading His people through tough times?

Go around the Fence

Let us strip off every weight that slows us down, especially the sin that so easily trips us up. And let us run with endurance the race God has set before us. We do this by keeping our eyes on Jesus, the champion who initiates and perfects our faith.

HEBREWS 12:1-2

Toward the end of spring training for my junior year of high school, the coaches determined that I was a better fit as an outside linebacker rather than middle.

As an outside backer, there were still times when I had to scrape, or take on blocks. However, my responsibility was different. Ultimately, the defense's goal is to force runners into as many defenders as possible. Inside linebackers clog the middle of the field and pursue from the center toward the sideline. The outside backer's job is to contain the ballcarrier, funneling him back toward the middle of the field.

One notable difference in pursuit for me as an outside linebacker was when the play went to the opposite side of the formation—for instance, if I were lined up closest to the left sideline, and the play went toward the right sideline. Dad explained to our group of five or six outside linebackers that in these situations he wanted us to "go around the fence" when pursuing a ballcarrier running to the opposite side of the field.

Dad explained that the middle of the field would most likely have lots of bodies that would block a clear path across the field to the ballcarrier. Also, if our teammates on the other side of the field were doing their job, the runner would most likely be funneled back to the middle. Going "around the fence" was Dad's term for getting around the obstacles that would prevent us from helping out if the runner cut back. Dad emphasized that our job was to get to the place the runner *could end up*, as there was no way to be there at the beginning of the play. This meant not getting tangled up in the stuff in the middle of the field.

In life we face innumerable distractions that may keep us from accomplishing our primary task. As we discussed in the previous reading, Paul faced numerous situations that could have become distractions for him. They were "scrape" opportunities where Paul had to go *through* these situations as a part of his calling. Yet Scripture teaches us that sometimes distractions are obstacles of our own making.

In my experience, many people, including me, tend to get distracted by good things. Many of these may even be things to which we are called. Work and ministry are two good activities that can become distractions if our eyes aren't fixed on the "champion who initiates and perfects our faith." When good things become an end in themselves, we are out of balance. Hobbies, leisure, and the like, while good and necessary, may sometimes take up too much of our time in light of our priorities. Sometimes these things may even tempt us to lower our standards so that we allow activities into our lives that don't build up our spiritual health. Learning to "go around the fence" can enable us to stay on task.

Let's ask God to direct our steps (see Proverbs 16:9) and show us the things that distract us from our goal of knowing and serving Him. Then, let's cast those aside, going around the fence toward our goal of knowing Jesus. As activities, obligations, and real life throw things our way this week, let's ask ourselves and our God whether these things are moving us toward Him.

TO GO DEEPER THIS WEEK . . .

» Read Proverbs 16:9.
» Read Hebrews 12:1-2.

1. Can you think of times (possibly now) when you allowed *good* things to become a hindrance to your relationship with God because they took on greater urgency or import than they should have? What were they? How did you recognize them? What did you do?

2. Can you think of a time when you (or someone you know) simplified life because busyness was preventing your living out your priorities? How were those priorities identified? How did the simplification take place? What steps did you or they take?

Two Whistles

If a soldier demands that you carry his gear

for a mile, carry it two miles.

MATTHEW 5:41

My dad was not a fan of average. He hated mediocrity. But he didn't measure good, bad, or average by the score of a game or the success of a given play. The effort and execution of the players was what he was looking for. Dad knew that sometimes a player would get beaten——that was just part of the game. What he couldn't abide was a lack of effort. Loafing wasn't tolerated. Lack of effort, to him, was a character issue. In Dad's words, "If you're going to do it, do it the best you can." This went beyond football or other sports, encompassing schoolwork, housework, yard work, and so on.

Dad had great means for determining a player's level of effort. Oftentimes, we'd do sprints across the width of the football field. If you were one of the faster players on the team and weren't near the front on the sprints, Dad would know that there were others giving more effort than you. Dad would check on his defensive players' effort by blowing his whistle at the end of a play. He would wait a couple of seconds and blow the whistle a second time. His expectation was that when he blew the whistle the second time, the defensive players should all be huddled around the downed ballcarrier. This meant that even if you weren't in on the play, you should be doing everything you could to get there to help. In an actual game, when the ball is still live, a play may look as though it has ended, when suddenly the running back bounces out of the pile. Hustling toward the play ensures that there is someone there to tackle him if that happens. If Dad caught a player lagging behind, the entire defense would pay for it with extra conditioning. His message in this was "Every player on the team will give 100 percent effort all the time. If you can't get there by the second whistle it must be because you are tired and are not conditioned well enough."

There are times in life when we are tempted to "take a play off," or to just go through the motions. As the monotony of day-to-day tasks wears on us, we lose perspective on the importance of excellence in everything we do. As Christians, I believe that we sometimes think certain daily responsibilities are more spiritual and merit more attention. But in reality, the distinction between the sacred (having to do with God) and the secular (having to do with the world) is not as clear cut as we may think. *All* that we do can be a means of worshiping and serving our Father. Paul says that whatever work we happen to be doing should be "all out," since in all we do we are serving Christ (see Colossians 3:23).

Keeping in mind Dad's words to me, "If you're going to do it, do it the best you can," I am learning that managing my time can be my primary challenge. The question about how hard to work is answered: "with all your heart" (Colossians 3:23, NIV). Our work ethic and the quality of our work may be the only things many people know of us. If they are less than our best, we aren't representing our God as we should. If we do excellent work, it may open doors and widen our potential sphere of influence (see 1 Peter 2:12; 1 Thessalonians 2:9; Proverbs 22:29).

This week let's ask our Father to give us wisdom to know how to spend our time. In the roles He has called us to, let's ask Him to give us supernatural energy and grace. It is only as we learn to know God better that we are able to truly work with all our heart in a way that brings honor to Him.

As we are strengthened by His power, we are enabled to give full effort through "the second whistle," knowing we are working for Him, not for man.

TO GO DEEPER THIS WEEK . . .
» Read Proverbs 22:29.
» Read Matthew 5:39-42.

» Read Colossians 1:10-11.
» Read Colossians 3:23-24.
» Read 1 Thessalonians 2:9.
» Read 1 Peter 2:12.

1. How might the effort you give in your work open doors for you to have an impact for God?
2. Write out what you would hope your boss, coworkers, friends, or family would say about you and the effort you put into the work that you are entrusted to do.

The Importance of Vision

When people do not accept divine guidance, they
run wild. But whoever obeys the law is joyful.

PROVERBS 29:18

Vision is a critical factor for a good running back. Can he see the entire field in context? Does he recognize blocks before they happen? Is he able to notice when defenders are overpursuing? Great backs usually have speed, agility, explosiveness, strength, and elusiveness. All of these qualities are a part of the package, but without great vision, all the raw talent in the world may result in a running back who performs at a lower level than his physical measurables would lead you to expect.

My dad took me aside as a junior high player and told me that it was important for me to know what every player on the team was supposed to be doing on a given play. Dad explained that knowing every role would help me understand *why* things happened on the football field. He was teaching me how to develop context for the game. I gained a much better idea of what *should* be occurring during each play. Dad was helping me develop great vision.

When I was a junior in high school, our top senior running back, a major college prospect, suddenly quit the team. Three games into the season, we needed to develop a different offensive identity. My role as fullback suddenly became more important. I would need to be more of a runner and not just a blocker. In my first game in this expanded role, it became apparent that despite lacking several of the usual innate talents of great backs—speed, explosiveness, and elusiveness—I was still an effective ball-carrier. I believe the reason for my effectiveness was my great field vision. One of my coaches joked that if I had more speed, I'd have been an All-American. I don't know about that, but I do know that my body didn't need great speed to find open field. My trained eyes led my body into it. (Since I was a step slow, this often just meant I'd have a really long run, only to be caught from behind on the ten-yard line!)

Vision is also critical in day-to-day life. Context and knowledge of how to play the game is crucial. God's Word has a lot to say about our playing field, and He wants us to read it to gain context for our lives. Maybe you have a particular talent or gift. You might be tempted at times to "talent" your way to your goals. But remember, even the fastest, quickest, strongest backs are limited if they don't have great vision. Conversely, average backs can sometimes do the spectacular *because* of great vision.

The story of Balaam illustrates moving forward without proper vision. Balaam had been offered money to go and curse the Israelites. Even as he traveled, an angel of the Lord was sent to direct his path. Apparently, despite his assertion that he would do only what God told him to do, Balaam's heart was set on something else. He wanted to go where he wanted to go, not necessarily where God was directing him. This angel came and blocked the path Balaam was trying to take. Balaam's donkey could see the angel and was trying to avoid him. Balaam, unable to see the angel, began to get really angry with his donkey! He proceeded to beat the poor animal. Finally, God opened Balaam's eyes so that he could see the angel. The angel told Balaam that the donkey's behavior had probably saved his life. Balaam repented and listened to the direction given to him by God through the angel. Only when Balaam's vision was restored could he see the right direction to go. Let's ask God to give us a clear vision for where He is leading us this week.

TO GO DEEPER THIS WEEK . . .
» Read Numbers 22.
» Read Proverbs 3:5-6.

1. What talents or skills do you have that you believe God wants you to use to fulfill His purposes for your life? List them. Ask God to give you a clear vision for how *He* would have you use them.
2. What are some things that may be obscuring your vision? Ask God to open your eyes to any barriers that are preventing you from having clear direction or vision from Him.

We, Not Me

*The human body has many parts, but the many parts
make up one whole body. So it is with the body of Christ.*

1 CORINTHIANS 12:12

O ver the years, "We, Not Me" has become the slogan
for a lot of sports teams. I'm not sure where it started,
but the first time I heard it was when my Dad coined the
phrase for one of his high school teams in the late 1980s.

There are twenty-two players on a football field at any
given time, each with his own individual role. A team
starts to become great when each of these individuals gives
up his identity for the sake of the team. Each player deter-
mines that the guys in that huddle with him are more
important than any personal glory he may achieve. It
requires great character and discipline to be a "We, Not
Me" player. A person with character knows that being a
part of something bigger than himself justifies setting personal goals and accolades aside for the sake of the team.

Discipline provides the player with the ability to stick to his assignment when his instinct may be to make the play himself. Particularly on defense, it can be difficult for him to stay in position, playing his role, as everything in him screams to just take off after the ballcarrier. However, "We, Not Me" means fulfilling his role so that another teammate can make the big play.

The old adage states, "It is amazing what you can accomplish if you do not care who gets the credit." This is so true in all of life, not just on a football field. Having a firm grasp of your own identity and role will determine how well you are able to give up personal credit for the team. In my work I have found that focusing on helping other people reach their goals, become their best, or find their purpose actually makes my work more fulfilling and successful. I had the remarkable privilege of working for the pharmaceutical giant Merck and Co., Inc. When I worked there, one of the core values of the company was to focus on the needs of the patients first. In 1950, the company's leader, George Merck, said, "We try never to forget that medicine is for the people. It is not for the profits. The profits follow, and if we have remembered that, they have never failed to appear. The better we have remembered it, the larger they have been." These words exemplify the "We, Not Me" mind-set in a corporate setting.

Scripture tells us that we, the church, are the body of

Christ. Bodies hug, bodies shake hands, and bodies sit with a weeping friend who has lost a loved one. Bodies bring dinner over to a family going through a crisis. Simply put, a body is how love is *physically* manifested. God loves us and tells us that the world will know us by our love for one another (see John 13:34-35). He also tells us that in His body, we have specific roles, and that the body doesn't function properly without each part working together (see 1 Corinthians 12:12-26).

A great team realizes that every member has his distinct role, without which the team will not be as successful. God has designed the church the same way. Whether you think you can contribute or not, God says you can—and *your church needs you*!

This week, let's ask God to show us how and where we fit in His body, the church. If you haven't been attending, make it a point to go. You are specifically designed to be an integral part of His body. God desires a personal relationship with you. And He has made it clear that part of knowing Him and yourself well involves being a part of His "We"—the church.

TO GO DEEPER THIS WEEK . . .
» Read John 13:34-35.
» Read 1 Corinthians 12:12-26.

1. What are specific areas within your local church where you may be able to contribute to the functioning of the body of Christ?

2. Think of a time when a Christian brother or sister has been there for you or someone you know with just what was needed at just the right time. Describe it. Ask for God to show you opportunities to be the answer to someone else's prayer.

Deliver the Blow

*Be strong in the Lord and in his mighty power. . . . Take
the sword of the Spirit, which is the word of God.*

EPHESIANS 6:10, 17

There is a scene in the movie *Woodlawn* where my dad, Coach Gerelds, pulls aside his young running back, Tony Nathan, and says, "This is a contact sport, okay? When someone wants to hit you, it feels good to hit 'em first, okay? Try it." The movie encapsulates in a few minutes Tony's journey from being the passive recipient of contact to being a powerful initiator (when necessary). In my book *Woodlawn*, I describe Tony's early days of playing football as a time when he was extremely contact shy. He was a skinny sophomore with incredible athletic ability, whom the coaches jokingly referred to as Chicken Little. When he filled out into a powerfully built yet still contact-shy football player, the coaches called him Chicken Big. Finally, Tony had an epiphany. He realized that, at times, contact was inevitable. At those times, it was a lot more fun, a lot less painful, and a lot more productive to be the one delivering the blow rather than the one taking it. At this point, Tony's nickname became simply Big.

My experience has taught me that oftentimes men run through life like Chicken Little. We are moving forward, but when difficulty arises and we face obstacles, we tend to absorb the blows rather than initiate according to our will and beliefs. I believe that God has designed us to be initiators. When God created the earth and all the plants, animals, and environmental conditions, His expectation—His command—was that we would subdue it. He didn't say that we would be subject to our environment and that whatever came our way would determine how our lives went. No, God intended for us to initiate (see Genesis 1:28).

When the serpent came to Adam and Eve and tempted them, had Adam fulfilled his God-given role as an initiator, he might have protected his wife from the evil intentions of the devil. Looking at Genesis 3:1-6, we see that Adam was *with* Eve, but he was passive. When the enemy came after Eve, Adam was present but didn't protect her. Even as Eve exaggerated what God had said (see Genesis 3:3), Adam stood by. Adam could have refuted Satan's lies with God's truth. God's Word is intended to defeat our enemy.

In Ephesians 6:10-17, Paul instructs us to put on the full armor of God. At the end of the passage he directs us to "take the sword of the Spirit, which is the word of

God" (verse 17). The rest of the armor Paul describes is defensive. Only the sword is an offensive weapon. God's Word is your sword.

This week as we live, work, love, and play, let us remember that God designed us to be initiators. Let us ask God to bring His Word to mind as our only offensive weapon against the schemes and lies that the enemy is telling us. The enemy may be a lion prowling about seeking to destroy you. But he has no power against the sword of the Spirit, God's Word. This week, when faced with an enemy who wants to hit you, hit 'im first with the Word of God.

TO GO DEEPER THIS WEEK . . .
» Read Genesis 1:28.
» Read Genesis 3:1-6.
» Read Ephesians 6:10-20.

1. Write a brief description of a situation in which someone taking the initiative made the difference between success and failure. (It doesn't have to be a spiritual or biblical story.)
2. What was the first Bible verse you memorized? What are some other verses you know? Do you have a plan for how to memorize passages? Investigate systems and methods for memorizing Scripture. (I find the *Topical Memory System Life Issues Memory Verse Cards* from the Navigators a helpful resource.)

Leave It All on the Field

My life has already been poured out as an offering to God. . . .
I have fought the good fight, I have finished the race,
and I have remained faithful.

2 TIMOTHY 4:6-7

When I played football for my father, each game's preparation began six days before, with Saturday treatment for any injuries. We followed up with Sunday film, light running, and stretching. Our two hardest days of work from a contact and conditioning standpoint would be Monday and Tuesday. We'd back off a bit on Wednesday and work on perfecting our execution in all three phases of the game (offense, defense, and special teams). Thursday would be a walk-through to make sure everyone knew his assignment and all of our communication was clear. Finally, Friday would arrive. School would end a little early so that we could have our pep rally. Many of us would have an early pregame meal together, then we'd gather at the field house to rest and get mentally focused for the game.

In football, when the clock hits 0:00 and the final whistle blows, it's too late to give another ounce of effort. It's over. Dad's encouragement to me and my teammates was to make sure that we made every second of practice *and* every second of that game count. We should pour ourselves out to accomplish what we set out to do. Dad would challenge us to "leave it all on the field." He wanted each player to make sure that all the effort and preparation that had gone into the preceding six days wasn't wasted. He knew that what we did during practice mattered.

As we walk through this life, the day-to-day grind may, at times, seem like drudgery. My experience in the corporate world has taught me that it is the simple faithfulness of daily doing with excellence the work I've been given that leads to spectacular results. It is *consistently* doing the seemingly mundane, unremarkable tasks that leads to stunning outcomes. In his book *The Slight Edge*, ultrasuccessful CEO, author, and speaker Jeff Olson says, "Successful people do what unsuccessful people are not willing to do."

But like the healing time on Saturday and the toil of the Sunday-to-Thursday lead-up to game time on Friday night, God is using our daily efforts to prepare us for eternity. God tells us in His Word that He is both preparing a *place* for us (see John 14:2-3) and preparing *us* to spend forever with Him (see Philippians 1:6).

God speaks to us through Paul as the apostle writes to

his son in the faith, Timothy. Paul knew what it meant to leave it all on the field. As we read in our opening verse, Paul fought the good fight, remained faithful, and finished the race. Paul's letters and the book of Acts only capture moments on his journey. There were many days of his life that were not recorded in the Bible. Still, it was his day-to-day obedience and *work* that led to his spectacular fight and race results.

As followers of Christ, we are called to leave it all on the field every day. As we discussed earlier, the work God has called you to is happening in the place He has called you to today. This week as we engage in the work we've been called to, let us keep in mind that we are fighting the fight, running the race, and keeping the faith, and that our Savior is preparing a place for us as God is preparing us for that place. When the clock hits 0:00 and the final whistle blows, let's make sure we've left it all on the field.

TO GO DEEPER THIS WEEK . . .

» Read John 14:2-3.
» Read Philippians 1:6.

1. Write your own obituary. What do you want your legacy to be? How do you want to be remembered?
2. What are some of the day-to-day actions you can take to help you live up to your desired legacy?

Givers and Takers

Don't be selfish; don't try to impress others. Be humble,
thinking of others as better than yourselves. Don't look out
only for your own interests, but take an interest in others, too.

PHILIPPIANS 2:3-4

Dad told me to look him in the eye as he said, "Son, there are givers and takers in the world. The takers are never happy. They are always wanting more. The givers' lives are fulfilling and happier as they seek to make things better for others." Dad became a Christian while he was coaching at Woodlawn High School, when I was just a little boy. Soon after his conversion, he began to stress to me the need to put others first. Dad modeled what it meant to be a giver in his work, both as a coach and later in the insurance industry. In the spring of 1984, Dad returned to football, accepting a position as head coach at Deshler High School in tiny Tuscumbia, Alabama. Suddenly, he wasn't just my dad, but since I was heading into my junior year of high school, he was now also my coach!

It didn't take Dad long to begin to share with his new team the things that were most important to him. Early on in the new job, Dad shared with his players the same message he'd given me almost a decade earlier. "Men, in life, you will find that there are givers and takers. You want to be a giver. Takers are always looking to *take* from people. They are always wondering if someone else is getting more than they are. Be a giver. Football is a game that requires you to give yourself up for the sake of the team. Being a giver will make you a better teammate. But more importantly, it will make you a better person. I am far more concerned with what kind of person you become than with what kind of football player you are." That team bought into this idea—slowly but surely. The first year was a bit rocky as a lot of individuals learned to be a team. A lot of spiritual transformation took place over the following years. Ultimately, a culture of givers developed on Dad's teams. This culture tended to expose the takers. Most of the time, those guys would either change or decide to do something else rather than play football.

As I've grown older, my dad's words have echoed true in every realm of my life. As a twenty-three-year-old man, I began dating my future wife, Jennifer. At that time, God put it on my heart to begin praying Philippians 2:3-4. God's Word tells us that we are not to conform to the way our culture acts, thinks, and believes, but instead to be transformed by the renewing of our minds (see Romans

12:2-5). I knew that apart from God's leading, I could easily behave just like our culture has trained me to think, looking out for number one. Selfishness is our natural inclination. When I asked God to help me live out the words in these verses, He began to transform me, helping me begin to put Jennifer's interests ahead of my own. Our twenty-plus years of marriage have allowed us to see God continue this transformation process.

Through Paul, God commanded the church at Philippi to be givers instead of takers. My dad had learned through years of playing sports, coaching sports, selling insurance, and being a husband and father that true peace and fulfillment could only be found as he put others first. My experience has taught me the same. As children, our natural inclination is one of selfishness. We come into the world as takers, completely dependent on our parents or caregivers. As we grow physically, God's design is that we also grow spiritually and emotionally, learning to move away from our childish, selfish ways and toward becoming givers.

This week, let's really focus on God's Word. The Bible teaches us to meditate on His Word day and night (see Psalm 1:1-3). The biblical definition of *meditation* is concentrated thinking about and pondering God's Word, turning it over and over in our minds and hearts. God desires us to allow Him to change the way we think, act, and believe. When we meditate on His Word, God uses it to transform our minds. Let's ask God to help us put away childish behaviors and reasoning. Let us ask our Father to help us put others first and find joy as He enables us to be givers rather than takers.

TO GO DEEPER THIS WEEK . . .
» Read Psalm 1:1-3.
» Read 1 Corinthians 13:11.
» Read Hebrews 5:11-14.

1. What are some practical actions you can take this week to be a giver rather than a taker? For your family? Friends? Coworkers? Others?
2. Can you think of a time you witnessed someone genuinely seeking to put others first, considering others' needs ahead of his or her own? What was the situation? What did that person do? How did other people respond? What was the outcome you observed?

PART 2

"Just about anyone can identify a problem.
What the world needs are more
problem solvers."

Loving versus Liking

Your love for one another will prove to the
world that you are my disciples.

JOHN 13:35

At my dad's funeral, I shared about the incredible love he had for people. I recounted a conversation I'd had with my father many years earlier. My dad and I had a lot of things in common, but our temperaments were quite different. One day as Dad was talking to me about our similarities and differences, he said something that I still laugh about, and yet it was quite profound as well. "Son, I wish I was more like you around people—the way you make everybody feel welcomed and like you're interested in them. Unfortunately, I just don't like people that much." My first thought was, *That hardly sounds like someone many would describe as bubbling over with love.* But then I started thinking about how nearly every one of his players would tell you that they played their hearts out for him because they *knew* that he *loved* them.

What I began to realize is that there is a big difference between loving and liking. Liking is easy. It requires no effort. You can like someone because they like the same sports team, the same music, or the same video games as you! Just enjoying being around someone is not love. These days, if you were to survey ten young men or women off the street and ask them how they knew they loved someone, I think the answers would vary. However, unless one of those people had a personal relationship with God through His Son, Jesus, I have an idea how some of the answers would sound. "She makes me want to be a better man." "I can't live without him." "She makes me feel better about myself." "He makes me feel safe." These are nice feelings, and many of them accompany love. However, they are not evidence of love.

Jesus set the bar pretty high when defining love. He told a religious leader of His day, "God so loved the world that he gave his one and only Son, that whoever believes in him shall not perish but have eternal life" (John 3:16, NIV).

God so loved the world that He *gave*. God's love inspired giving up something, rather Someone, of great value for us, the objects of His love. Love equals giving. Jesus then goes further and says that true love is "to lay down one's life for one's friends" (John 15:13). Then

Jesus commands His followers to follow His example (see John 13:34-35).

Jesus wants us to love "just as I have loved you" (John 13:34). How did He love us? By laying His life down for us. So now He is commanding us to love in the same way. His words have laid out for us a very specific call to self-sacrificial, *life-giving* love. First, we are told that the Father, *because He loved, gave.* Second, Jesus emphasizes how *He will show His love* to His disciples. Third, Jesus makes it clear that *we are to love one another as He loved us.* How did He love us? By giving His life up for us.

As we interact with friends, neighbors, and family this week, let's look for opportunities to love as Christ did. We won't necessarily be called to lay our lives down in physical death. But we are to look for areas where we can die to our own desires for the sake of those we love. Jesus made it clear that His kind of love is solid evidence that you are His disciple. Our world is looking for the real, the true. This Christlike love is not natural. It is supernatural. This week, let's ask the Father to give us opportunities to share His love with others. Let's seek to move beyond liking, which is easy for most of us. Instead, let's go deeper, to loving like Jesus did. People will notice. And God will be honored.

TO GO DEEPER THIS WEEK . . .
» Read John 13:34-35.
» Read John 15:13.

1. What are some ways you can show love to those in your family (or your roommates) this week? Be specific.
2. Think of someone in your life who really makes you feel loved. Describe why you feel this way and how they show you their love.

Knowing the Whys

If someone asks about your hope as a
believer, always be ready to explain it.

1 PETER 3:15

In March of 1984, Dad and I made a 115-mile move from rural Trussville, Alabama, to equally rural Tuscumbia, Alabama, for Dad's new coaching job. Before the move, he had already begun to study film of the young men who would be entrusted to him. Since I was going to be a part of the team, Dad had me watch film with him. I was a good athlete but not a great one. As I watched the images flickering on our dining room wall, I could see that many of my future teammates were better athletes than me. Still, Dad believed that knowledge was power. He knew that if I knew exactly what he was looking for, I could probably get the job done with my abilities. Therefore, my father began to teach me as much as my fifteen-year-old brain could take in about almost every position on the field.

Dad wanted me to know my job and my teammates' jobs. He wanted me to know *why* things happened on the football field. He explained to me that the more I knew about why things happened, the more I'd develop a mastery of the game. You often hear people talk about players always being at the right place at the right time. Dad contended that this wasn't by accident. He taught me that knowing the game allowed players to play at a level beyond many others with superior athletic ability. I enjoyed all that I absorbed from him that spring, but I didn't really realize the impact of it until September 28, nearly six months after our inaugural spring training at Deshler High School.

We had lost our top tailback for the season the week before. As a result, the coaches moved the starting fullback to tailback and moved me into the starting fullback role. That night, I had the opportunity to run the ball in a varsity game for the first time. Everything that I'd been taught over the previous years and months suddenly allowed me to see lanes opening before they opened. The knowledge of *why* things were happening had made me into a better football player. I'd love to say that we beat the best team in the area that night and I was carried off the field as a hero. That didn't happen. However, Deshler played toe-to-toe with the area champion and nearly knocked them off. And I came away appreciating how much knowing the why could make a difference in my performance.

Years later, as a young adult, I was challenged once again

about the importance of knowing the whys. God allowed me to go through some very tough times. It was during these years that I began to battle depression. Part of how the depression played out in my life was through challenges to my faith. Doubt dogged me daily. But God moved me to dig in and to build a strong foundation for why I believe what I believe. Keep in mind, there are things God has called us to simply trust Him with, whys for which we will never know the answers this side of eternity. That said, God has called us to love Him with all our heart, soul, *mind*, and strength (see Matthew 22:37). God never intended for Christians to check our minds at the church door.

The world we live in today is filled with people who have been raised to doubt the scriptural truth that Jesus is God's Son or that God even exists. There is a not-so-subtle idea in our culture that belief in Jesus and God's amazing redemptive story are for those who haven't checked the facts. I believe that God is calling us to overcome this perception. As I shared earlier, He has called us to speak the truth in love (see Ephesians 4:15). God has also instructed us to know the whys of our faith.

God teaches us through the apostle Peter to always be ready to give the *reason* for our hope (see 1 Peter 3:15). With his admonition to share our faith with gentleness and respect (verse 16), Peter echoes Paul's instructions to the Ephesians to do so lovingly.

This week, let's invest some time in learning of our

own reasons for the hope that is in us. God desires for us to grow in our ability to engage those in our culture with answers to the whys in their lives.

TO GO DEEPER THIS WEEK . . .

» Read Matthew 22:37.
» Read Ephesians 4:15.
» Read 1 Peter 3:15.

1. Have there been times in your Christian life when you struggled with doubt about some aspect of your faith? What was it? What did you do?

2. This week, look for resources to help you develop a good, rational basis for your faith. These can be video series, books, CDs, podcasts, websites, and so on. Some books that have benefited me are *Mere Christianity* (C. S. Lewis), *More Than a Carpenter* (Josh McDowell), *Evidence That Demands a Verdict* (Josh McDowell), *The Verdict of History* (Gary Habermas), *Who Moved the Stone?* (Frank Morison), *A Shattered Visage* (Ravi Zacharias), *Scaling the Secular City* (J. P. Moreland), *I Don't Have Enough Faith to Be an Atheist* (Norman Geisler and Frank Turek), *The Case for Christ* (Lee Strobel), *The God Who Is There* (Francis Schaeffer), *Reasonable Faith* (William Lane Craig), and *Darwin's Black Box* (Michael Behe).

No Excuses

Overwhelming victory is ours through Christ, who loved us.

ROMANS 8:37

I began to play competitive sports at a very young age and continued to compete throughout my growing-up years—in baseball, football, track, wrestling, and swimming. From the very beginning of my experience in sports, Dad emphasized how important it was to take responsibility for my own actions. He taught me that my results were on me. He wouldn't tolerate excuses. However, as a boy and as a young man, I wanted desperately to please my dad and make him proud. In my mind, finding reasons for my slipups, gaffes, or oversights would keep Dad from being disappointed in me. I soon found out that he wasn't nearly as bothered by my mistakes or failures as he was by my response to them. Dad didn't want me to develop "victim thinking," the tendency we all have at times to believe that our circumstances dictate our outcomes.

Dad practiced what he preached as well. As a coach, if his team lost, he always said it was his fault. I watched him do this in games where it was obvious that a missed call or a fluky play might have made the difference in a game. It would have been easy for him to allow these things to be "reasons" his team didn't win. But he would have no part in that. Dad never saw himself as a victim. Instead, he saw himself as someone to whom God had given a mission to accomplish, regardless of circumstances.

Earlier in my adult life, I managed sales in four states for a pharmaceutical company. I worked with outstanding reps across the southeastern United States. One of our team's core values was that we wouldn't make excuses. I explained to my teammates what I had learned from my dad. Excuses just waste time. If a mistake is made, or expected results don't occur, it really doesn't matter whose fault it is, or what circumstances may have contributed to the shortfall. What *does* matter is what we are going to do to fix it. My team understood that just about anyone can *identify* a problem. What the world needs are more problem *solvers*. Problem identifiers are victims of circumstances. When we become problem solvers, we become empowered to use the abilities God has given us to be change agents in the world around us.

Writing to the Christian believers in Rome, Paul

addresses this deep human desire to avoid condemnation and blame. It's natural to want to justify or validate ourselves. But God invites us to a deeper honesty—the freedom in Christ to admit failure, knowing He accepts and loves us regardless of our performance. From this position of strength even in exposed weakness, we have confidence—confidence to rest in the completed work of Christ that declares us worthy, and confidence to move forward toward potential growth opportunities. We can quit casting blame and pursue solutions instead.

This week, let's meditate on the finished work of Jesus. Focus on the fact that you are deeply loved by the Father. Nothing—nothing—*nothing* can separate you or me from the love of our Father. Inevitably, we will make mistakes this week. Let us ask God to make us problem solvers, rejecting the lies of the Accuser, so that we can be His change agents in this world.

TO GO DEEPER THIS WEEK . . .
» Read Romans 8:31-38.

1. Are there times when it is difficult for you to admit you were wrong? In what type of situations is this most common? Why do you think this is?
2. Ask God to show you areas where you are clinging to your own record rather than resting in the knowledge that God loves you just as you are. Confess these

areas and then let them go. You may even consider speaking to a friend or mentor about these areas specifically, as God sometimes uses our confessions and openness to free us from sin.

A Proper Handshake

The churches in the province of Asia send you greetings.

Aquila and Priscilla greet you warmly in the Lord,

and so does the church that meets at their house.

1 CORINTHIANS 16:19, NIV

When I was a very young boy, probably around four years old, my dad began to teach me how to give a proper handshake. Dad would lean down so I could look him in the eye. He would extend his hand to me, his much larger hand basically enveloping mine. Dad told me to be firm, but not to squeeze too hard. "Don't have a dead-fish handshake, but don't break their hand. Just let 'em know you're there." As the years went by, Dad would introduce me to grown men, and I did as I was taught. I knew he expected it, and I could tell he was pleased that his little boy knew how to respectfully meet and greet grown-up men.

Many of Dad's players came from homes where no father was present, and he became a surrogate dad for

67

them. He would go player by player on his teams to ensure that each young man was taught how to give a proper handshake. Just as he did with me, he would look each player in the eye and ask the player to look him in the eye. He would teach each one how long and how firmly to hold the handshake, and even how to place his hand. He'd caution the players not to grab too soon and cut someone's handshake off short, grabbing only his or her fingers. A proper handshake is like two puzzle pieces fitting together. The hands slide into position as the thumbs align next to each other. Then the firm, not painful, squeeze—eyes locked on the eyes of your acquaintance or friend.

Why did my dad make such a big deal about a proper handshake? I believe it had to do with respect. He believed in showing appropriate respect to everyone. He also believed that a man should behave in a way that inspires respect. Jesus taught that the little things matter (see Luke 16:10). Dad believed that too. A handshake was a simple step in the right direction for a young man wanting to establish himself as someone to be respected.

Throughout the book of Romans, Paul communicates greetings to and from various brothers and sisters more than twenty times (see Romans 16:1-16 for examples). That's a lot of hellos and handshakes. Paul's instructions on these greetings make them seem like little things. But were they really?

When we start looking closely at Paul's greetings, a couple of things become clear:

1. Paul used his greetings to show he valued the person he greeted.
2. Paul used his greetings to encourage the person he greeted.

When my dad taught me and others on his team how to give an appropriate handshake, it freed us to look for ways to encourage others when we greeted them. How many times do we meet people and immediately forget their names? Let's keep in mind Paul's purpose for greetings: to encourage and value the one greeted.

This week as we greet our friends, let's shake hands, but let's also look for ways to convey how much we value them and to encourage them in their walk with God. As we meet new acquaintances, let us seek ways to affirm them through our greetings. The proper handshake can be the first step—the right start to potentially life-giving relationships. We want to impact others' souls with respect and godly encouragement.

TO GO DEEPER THIS WEEK . . .
» Read Luke 16:10.
» Read Romans 16:1-16.

1. Why do you think we sometimes forget people's names immediately after we're introduced to them?

2. Here are a couple of practical things you can do this week to encourage and show respect to others: (1) Repeat someone's name back to them in conversation after meeting them; (2) take a moment to write a letter and send it by snail mail to someone you care about just to encourage them.

Characteristics of a Winner

*Jesus grew in wisdom and in stature and in
favor with God and all the people.*

LUKE 2:52

In coaching his football teams, Dad had a system for
looking at the total person as a potential football
player. In football, the easiest thing for anyone to look
at is athletic ability—and that is an important component. However, my father felt that athletic ability must
be matched with a couple of other important factors in
order for a player to be a winner for the team. Dad's three
primary criteria were:

1. Character
2. Football intelligence
3. Athletic ability

In order to truly evaluate his players, Dad really had to
get to know them. He watched and listened. He learned a

lot by how players interacted with one another. If a player was respected by his teammates, it would show up in how they responded to him. Other teachers in the school also contributed to a player's overall character profile. Athletic ability and football intelligence were determined by on-the-field performance. Dad would ballpark a kid's rating from one to ten on each of these characteristics. There aren't a whole lot of "ten" athletes in rural Alabama high school football. So most of the kids on the team would have to make up for their lack of innate athletic ability with intelligence and character.

What Dad understood is that each of his players had a ceiling on athletic ability. Coaching could only help them improve so far. What Dad *could* affect the most was a player's character and football intelligence. Players can grow in character, knowledge, and skill. These are things that can be learned and honed. Dad's goal was to have a team full of "twenty-fives." So if he had a "six" athlete, he'd work to develop him into a "ten" in character and a "nine" in football intelligence.

All of us are innately gifted. Some have outstanding athletic ability. Some have outstanding intellectual capacity. Some have an innate sense of people, what some call emotional IQ. Most have more moderate gifting in each of these areas. All of us are charged with growing and maximizing these gifts. That's where character comes in. Growth requires hard work. Hard work requires character.

My own experience with working to develop people in the business world has shown me that everyone is gifted in different ways. And I've found that people with differing levels of natural giftedness can be equally successful as they develop those parts of their whole person that can be improved. Jesus taught His disciples about this principle in Matthew 25:14-30. In this parable Jesus tells of a man who went on a journey. While he was gone, he entrusted three of his servants with differing amounts of money. He gave one servant five bags of silver; another, two bags; and the third, one bag. The master's expectation was that each man would use the resources he'd been given to their fullest extent. When the man returned, he praised the first two servants, who had doubled the money he'd left with them. However, he was not pleased with the servant who'd been given one bag of silver because this servant had done nothing to *improve* the resources he'd been given.

God has given you everything you need for a successful life—as measured by His standards. You may be extraordinarily talented in your field, or you may be less talented than some. Regardless of your innate talent level, God expects you to grow in the areas where you can develop. Even Jesus grew in wisdom and stature, and in favor with God and man (see Luke 2:52). We are called to do the same. This week, let's ask God to show us areas we can work on, grow in, and develop as we seek to be the winners He has created us to be.

TO GO DEEPER THIS WEEK . . .

» Read Matthew 25:14-30.

1. What are some specific character areas you'd like to grow in? Look over the fruits of the Spirit listed in Galatians 5:22-23, and ask God to develop in you some of those particular qualities this week.

2. Think through areas where God has given you natural talents. Consider how those talents could be used to serve in your local church. Talk with someone in your church or with a mentor about how you can maximize the talents God has given you for the sake of others.

The Little Things Matter

If you are faithful in little things, you will be faithful
in large ones. But if you are dishonest in little things,
you won't be honest with greater responsibilities.

LUKE 16:10

My dad had just gone through his instructions for the quarterbacks for the third time. Russ Cleveland, the starting quarterback, and his backup, Bo Horton, stood attentively listening and watching as Dad took the snap. Then, in his own version of slow motion, Dad walked through opening the hips and reversing out. He repeated it to make sure they knew exactly how he wanted them to do it. When you watch quarterbacks practicing in clips on television or the Internet, you often see the emphasis the coaches put on their footwork when they are dropping back to pass. A quarterback needs to set his feet well and have a good foundation (remember how important our foundation is!) to be able to throw effectively. In the moment I'm describing, Dad was going through this precise footwork over and over just to make sure the quarterbacks were *handing the ball off* appropriately. That's right. Dad wanted precise, repeatable perfection on his offense's handoffs. This is only one of hundreds of examples I could give about the importance of the little things to my dad when it came to executing his offense.

Dad's obsessive focus on the small details of running his offense makes me smile and think of the times he stayed on me about doing things the right way. I'd be all exasperated—the way I see my own daughters responding to me at times! But as I've grown older, I've realized that there is something to this idea. The movie *Woodlawn*, based on the true story captured in my book by the same name, contains an example of God using the little things as the final push for my dad to become a Christian. In one scene, there is a Fellowship of Christian Athletes meeting at a home in an upper-middle-class, white neighborhood called Crestwood. The movie captures the fact that Dad was concerned that the black athletes wouldn't feel welcome in that neighborhood.

What the movie didn't go into was that a few families had decided against having the meeting at their home. We can't be sure of their motivation, but what we can know is that the Miller family decided that they *would* host the meeting because they believed the Bible taught them that, as Christians, they should be hospitable. This small decision to obey what they'd read in the Bible probably didn't seem like that big of a deal to them. But for my dad, it was the thing that brought everything together. Dad saw a *white* family loving all people just the same. The Miller family didn't behave any differently toward any of the players. They loved them all. Dad realized he didn't have the same kind of love in his heart that the Millers had. He slipped out the door as soon as the meeting ended and drove home. While driving, he prayed—that is, he talked out loud to God. He told Him that he wanted to be able to love like the Millers loved. He asked for God to come into his life and to change him and to give him a love for others. And God did. My dad's life changed from that day forward.

In today's verse, Jesus tells His disciples that the person who is faithful in the very little things is faithful also in big things. And the person who is unfaithful in the little things is unfaithful also in the big things. Jesus lets us know that the little things matter!

This week, let's purpose to do everything to the very best of our ability. Let's ask God to use our obedience in the little things.

TO GO DEEPER THIS WEEK ...
» Read Deuteronomy 7:22.
» Read Matthew 13:31-32.
» Read Luke 12:2-3.

1. Can you think of a time when someone did a little thing that made a difference for you? What was it? Why do you think it had the impact it did?
2. What are some "little things" you can do this week to convey love to others?

Something Worth Cheering

Anyone who belongs to Christ has become a new person.
The old life is gone; a new life has begun!

2 CORINTHIANS 5:17

In 1973, there was an amazing spiritual transformation going on within my dad's Woodlawn High School football team. As Dad watched Jesus knock down racial barriers and replace hate and fear with love, he, too, started a relationship with Him. Before his conversion, Dad says he didn't know how to love. But after experiencing God's forgiveness and acceptance, he was freed up to love without restraint. He was no longer captive to his own fears and insecurities. I'm not saying that Dad didn't still deal with lingering issues—we all do. But those who accept God's forgiveness and start a relationship with Him know that there is a definite weight lifted and freedom felt as God wipes away their record of sin and separation from Him. God literally recreates us!

As Dad's life changed, he grew in gratitude, affection, and devotion to God. He really wanted to cheer about what God had done in his life. He wanted others to share in the excitement he had for the freedom he had found.

In 1974, Woodlawn played Banks High School. The game was memorable because it featured what most people considered the two best high school teams in the football-crazy state of Alabama. It also featured two of the nation's most highly touted college prospects. Banks quarterback Jeff Rutledge was one of the very best at his position, and Woodlawn's "Touchdown Tony" Nathan was one of the nation's top running back prospects. Yet what Dad remembered most about that night wasn't the amazing athletes or even the game itself. Instead, he was blown away by how many fans in the record crowd of 42,000 filling Birmingham's Legion Field held signs celebrating their relationship with God. The transformation that had started at Woodlawn the previous fall had spread throughout the school and even down First Avenue North to their biggest rival. For years afterward, Dad told stories of the banners around the stadium that displayed the excitement people had about the freedom they had found in a relationship with God. He would say, "Man, I wish we'd get as excited about Jesus as we do about these football games." Dad was passionate about football. But he knew that football was no match for the work God has done or for who God is.

Being that excited about God was challenging to me. It still is. Recently, I was reading a book called *Fresh Air* by my own pastor, Chris Hodges. In it, Chris notes that the word translated as *praise* in English Bibles could come from one of seven different words in the original Hebrew. One of those words is *hallel*. Pastor Hodges shares that "*hallel* means 'to boast,' 'to rave,' 'to celebrate,' even to be 'clamorously foolish.'"[1] If you're like me, you may have wondered, *So what does the word* hallelujah *mean? Jah* means God. So the word *hallelujah* literally means to boast, rave, celebrate, or be clamorously foolish about God. Growing up in a football culture, I've seen lots of boasting, raving, celebrating, and even clamorous foolishness from fans and have done some myself. My dad would've never called himself a biblical scholar, but it seems he did have insight into what true praise looks like.

It may still seem a bit unnatural to many of us to get *that* excited about God. I know that I sometimes wonder why I'm not more excited about Him. But I also *know* that He loves me. I am a work in progress, and so are you. This week, let's ask God to give us an excitement about Him and what He is doing in us. Let's ask Him to help us recognize the great gift He has given us. As He does this, we will come to a place where we realize that who He is and what He has done are things worth cheering.

---

[1]Chris Hodges, *Fresh Air* (Carol Stream, IL: Tyndale, 2012), 119.

TO GO DEEPER THIS WEEK...
- » Read Psalm 150.
- » Read Luke 19:35-40.

1. Try to come up with a list of twenty-six characteristics of God, one starting with each letter of the alphabet. Spend some time praising God for these attributes.
2. What are some things that you get *really* excited about? How do you express your excitement? Ask God to create in you a heart that overflows with joy, praise, and gratitude for who God is and what He has done for you.

Better Plays Don't Win Football Games

Observe people who are good at their work—
skilled workers are always in demand and admired;
they don't take a backseat to anyone.

PROVERBS 22:29, MSG

"It's really a very simple game," Dad said more times than I can count. "If each man whips his man, you win." Dad believed that if you blocked better, tackled better, executed better, and limited mistakes, you'd probably win the football game. He hated the idea of trying to outscheme, outsmart, or outguess his way to victory. No—hard work and good execution were the keys to winning.

In football, the defense always has at least one player who is not blocked. There are eleven players on offense and eleven players on defense. But on offense, one player is carrying the football, so that's one fewer blocker. If the quarterback hands the ball off to the running back, that's one fewer blocker. On pass plays, any player out on a pass route is one fewer blocker. But on defense, all eleven players can make the tackle. Good football plays have always been about leveraging this disparity of blockers to tacklers.

The bottom line in football is that every play has the potential to score. The success or failure of most plays has far less to do with the play call itself and more to do with the execution and physical abilities of the players on the field. There have definitely been innovators in football, but even the newest big offensive evolutions are most often changes in appearance rather than changes in the substance of what occurs once the ball is snapped.

Great coaches who experience sustained success are much more focused on developing excellence in what they and their teams do. "You may know what we're gonna do, but you still gotta stop us." Dad used to say that there were no shortcuts to success.

My experience in the business world has been the same. There are no tricks to sustained success. It comes as a result of doing the right things the right way. Changing football plays is often like changing the packaging of a product. You aren't changing the actual product. Success in business means you seek to provide a quality product to your customers in an ethical and professional manner. If you outwork your competitors and provide a superior product or excellent service, you will probably win more than you lose.

The Bible has innumerable examples of individuals

who were people of excellence and hard work. In Daniel 6:3, we learn that "because of Daniel's great ability," he was distinguished above all others in similar roles. His excellence brought him to the point that the king was planning to set him over the whole kingdom!

Winning in life, like winning in football games, doesn't come from reinventing the wheel. It comes from consistently acting with excellence and working hard. Excellence is related to hard work, but has more to do with *who* you are becoming and *how* you go about your work. Basically, living a life of excellence has to do with your character. Ask God to build excellence into your life. Confess to Him that it isn't new plays or new systems that will win in your life. It is only as He creates a *new you* that real winning will happen.

TO GO DEEPER THIS WEEK...
» Read Daniel 6.
» Read Galatians 5:22-23.

1. Describe what excellence in your field of work (or study) looks like to you.
2. What are some things you can do to further develop excellence as a lifestyle?

Follow Your Blocks

[The Lord] leads me beside peaceful streams. . . .

He guides me along right paths.

PSALM 23:2-3

"Stay on the guard's hip!" Dad would tell his tailback. "Follow your blocks!" On any play, the offensive line will have blocking assignments. Defenses may line up in multiple fronts, coverages, and alignments, so these assignments are often called out by the center to the rest of the linemen before the quarterback calls the snap count. When the blocks are carried out appropriately, the back should find a seam, or gap, between defensive players. Sometimes this gap or seam is referred to as the hole. The running back is expected to explode through this hole left by his blockers clearing out the area.

Dad's teams were famous for their amazing execution of the Wing-T offense. The series of plays that produced the bulk of their yards and touchdowns was called the

Buck Series. The Buck looks a bit like today's Jet Sweep. The tailback takes the handoff, running parallel to the line of scrimmage. Dad's team had both guards pulling to lead the tailback around the end. Going to the right was called 28 Buck, and to the left was 27 Buck. The numeral 2 represented the tailback. The 7 and 8 represented the gaps outside the tight ends. On 28 Buck, the two guards would take off toward the 8 gap, running parallel to the line of scrimmage. When they got to the outside of the tight end, they'd turn upfield. The playside guard would turn inside and seal off the linebacker. The offside guard would turn upfield and look for the first person to show, then he would "kick" him out. The tailback would stay on the outside hip of the deepest guard. When the guard engaged the defender, the tailback was to explode through the gap created between the two guards.

One of the things I appreciate most about the game of football is that there is a real *order* to it. You don't have to wonder, *Where do I go?* Plays are designed with a blocking scheme that makes it clear where you should run. Sure, the running back needs to develop a feel for how the blocks will develop. But when plays are executed properly, it's easy to see where to run. You simply *follow your blocks.*

How often have you wondered in real life where you were supposed to go or what you were supposed to do? I know I have wondered these things. There are decisions about which school to attend, how to spend my money, where to live, what career I'm supposed to pursue, how to parent correctly . . . The list could go on and on.

Fortunately, God hasn't left us alone in figuring out the answers to all these questions. God describes Himself as a Shepherd and us as His sheep. Sheep are instinctive "flockers"—they have a need to be with other sheep. If one sheep moves, the others will follow. Sometimes this leads to disastrous results. A Turkish newspaper reported that some shepherds left their herd grazing while they went to eat breakfast. They returned to find that 1,500 sheep had followed an initial sheep in jumping off a cliff! (Amazingly, the death toll was only 450 animals, as a fluffy white pile formed, cushioning the landing of over 1,000 of the sheep.)

Human beings often share these flocking instincts with sheep. We are known to follow other people's lead even when it isn't to our benefit. We need our Shepherd to guide us along right paths, like a blocker making a gap for a running back.

This week, as you make your plans, keep in mind that you have a Good Shepherd who leads the way. We need our leader to show us where we are supposed to go. Let's ask our Good Shepherd to give us wisdom as we plan. We have the Holy Spirit, God's Word, and Christian mentors to assist us as we seek His guidance. We can then "follow our blocks" as we allow Him to give us direction on each of the decisions we face.

TO GO DEEPER THIS WEEK . . .

» Read John 14–16.
» Read Psalm 23.

1. Are you facing any major decisions right now? If so, how do you plan to "follow your blocks," or find God's way through?

2. What are some ways you may sometimes "get ahead of your blocks" in your decision-making process?

That and
Twenty-Five Cents

You must all be quick to listen, slow to speak,
and slow to get angry.

JAMES 1:19

Football is an extremely passionate subject, particularly in certain regions, like the South and the Midwest. As a result, there is a *lot* of talk about it. Innumerable radio shows spend the bulk of their airtime with hosts, guests, and callers sharing their opinions about college and NFL football. As passionate as fans are, though, for most people football is just a pastime, a hobby. This wasn't true for Dad. Football was his job. He took it very seriously. He felt an enormous obligation to give his players the very best opportunity to win. Because it was so important to him, Dad didn't really enjoy opinion-based discussions of football. He preferred meaningful conversations with people who knew the game well and who might be able to help him do his job better.

As a talkative teenager with a passion for football, I had to learn how to have good conversations about the game with my dad. One day I was trying to get him to speculate about a particular Auburn game. Dad told me that it was a waste of time to speculate when you had no real insights into the various factors that could impact the outcome. Frustrated at not getting the answers I wanted from him, I gave him my thoughts. He answered, "Great, Son. That and twenty-five cents will get you a cup of coffee." The amazingly cheap price of a cup of coffee aside, Dad's point was that in many situations, opinions have no real value. That's not to say that people should never share their opinions. There are some topics on which sharing your opinions is valuable or socially responsible. However, speculation and opinion on certain topics and with certain people won't be appreciated and may actually be inappropriate.

The older I get, the more I realize that my dad's thoughts on opinions and speculation were rooted in wisdom. Oftentimes speculation and opinion are the source of disagreement and argument. As a believer, I've had to learn that my words can either bring blessings or curses to those with whom I interact (see James 3:10).

Jesus' brother James spends a great deal of time in his letter speaking about the tongue. He talks about the amazing power we have in such a small part of our body. I have had to learn that my desire to speak has to be tempered by keeping the listener's good in mind. As we learn to "speak the truth in love" (Ephesians 4:15), we are able to follow Jesus' command to be salt and light in a world in desperate need of both (see Matthew 5:13-15). Think about those analogies. What does salt do? It preserves and seasons food. What does light do? It overcomes darkness. It reveals things.

This week, let's ask God to give us wisdom to know how and when to speak. Far more than being a useless addition to our coffee money, our words are intended to bring truth, life, and love to those in our lives. Let's ask God to help us be the salt and light we were created to be.

TO GO DEEPER THIS WEEK . . .
» Read Matthew 5:13-15.
» Read Ephesians 4:15.
» Read James 1:19-20, 26.
» Read James 3:1-12.

1. What are some circumstances in which you find it difficult to control your tongue?
2. Why do you think you struggle in these situations? Ask God to help you to have self-control when faced with these challenges.

The Value of a Friend

Two people are better off than one,
for they can help each other succeed.

ECCLESIASTES 4:9

Growing up on Kawanda Lane in 1970s Birmingham was an amazing blessing. All the parents looked out for all the children. We played outside year-round, only going inside when the streetlight came on each night. The joy of those days was tied directly to the fact that I was blessed with really good friends. My best friends back then were Chris, Walt, and Scott. We played kick the can, hide-and-seek, baseball, street hockey, and football. We rode bikes, we built clubhouses, we just played. It was the epitome of innocence.

During that same time period, my family used to go on vacation with my dad's best friend and his family. Gary and Dad grew up together and loved each other deeply. Gary and his wife, Betty, and his two daughters, Lisa and

Michelle, were just like family to us. There was nothing that Gary or Dad wouldn't do for each other. They'd had a lifetime of memories together, and each knew that he could count on the other. Because of the nature of the coaching profession, I think that my dad didn't feel like he had the opportunity to make many friends. He was very close to his assistant coaches, but he rarely allowed himself to get really close to players' parents, as he didn't want anyone to think he was playing favorites. That's what made Dad's relationship with Gary so special. Their relationship preceded his days as a coach. Their shared history made the relationship deep. They enjoyed the more surface-level things, like football and hobbies, but they were able to go much deeper. Next to my mom and us kids, I think Dad was closer to Gary than anyone else in the world.

In 1977, I was finishing third grade. Dad had gotten out of coaching and was selling insurance. There was a lot of change happening. In addition to the career change, that year we moved to another town. My mom, my sisters, and I began to build new friendships. Meanwhile, Dad's best friend had gotten very sick. We would often drive down to Montgomery, where Gary and his family lived. Dad wanted to spend as much time with him as he could. Sadly, Gary wouldn't live through 1977. Dad was with Gary when he died, and he then drove to pick up Gary's youngest daughter, Michelle, from school to break the news to the brokenhearted fifteen-year-old. Dad had been Gary's best friend throughout lots of fun times and through the really tough times, all the way to the end. I learned a bit about what true friendship looks like by watching the two of them.

As I grew older and developed new relationships, I remember my dad emphasizing to me what a blessing it is to have good friends. Dad would hold his hand up with all fingers extended and say, "If you can count five people as true friends, you should consider yourself extremely blessed." Dad's definition of a true friend was based on his own experience with friendship and with having been blessed with a great friend. As I grew up, God blessed me with truly amazing friends that I knew would be with me through anything. Many of them *have* gone with me through amazingly good and excruciatingly tough times. Chip, Tommy, Jerry, Jimbo, Andy, Bill, Lew, Kye, Chris, Al, Hugh, Jeff, Kyle, Phillip, William. So many names—and I could list many more. God has put so many different people in my life during different seasons. My wife, Jennifer, and I have been through so many great, fun times together. But she has also gone through agonizing times with me.

The Bible tells us an amazing story of true friendship in 1 Samuel. Jonathan was Saul's son, but David had been chosen by God to succeed Saul as king of Israel. David and Jonathan formed a covenant by which Jonathan would be second in command in Israel when David became king, and David would protect Jonathan and his family. Their friendship demonstrated selflessness, loyalty, open and honest communication, and sacrificial love for each other rather than envy. They always looked out for each other, whatever the cost.

We also learn in the Bible that God considers us blessed when we have friends who are there to help us through tough times (see Ecclesiastes 4:9-12). The essential component to any *true* friendship is knowing Jesus as the Friend who sticks closer than a brother (see Proverbs 18:24). We learn in John 15:13 that Jesus demonstrated the ultimate act of true friendship when He laid down His life for us.

This week, let's thank our Father in heaven for giving His Son to be our best Friend. Let's also thank Him for those He has brought into our lives as friends and ask Him to help us be true friends to them in all we do. Additionally, let's ask God to send us true friends. Let us ask Him to bring people into our lives who love Him first and therefore are people who are able to truly love someone as a friend.

TO GO DEEPER THIS WEEK . . .
» Read 1 Samuel 18:1-4.
» Read Proverbs 18:24.
» Read Ecclesiastes 4:9-12.
» Read John 15:13.

1. Why do you think we are sometimes reluctant to talk about deeper issues and instead focus only on sports, weather, politics, etc.?

2. What are some ways you can deepen your friendships with the people God has put in your life?

Evidence of a Life Well Lived

We keep on praying for you, asking our God to enable you to live a life worthy of his call. May he give you the power to accomplish all the good things your faith prompts you to do.

2 THESSALONIANS 1:11

My mom was in Perkasie, Pennsylvania, visiting (and helping!) my wife, Jennifer, and me. We'd just had our third daughter, Alli. Our older two daughters, Morgan and Bailey Kay, were four and three years old respectively. We were overjoyed at the arrival of Allison Taylor Gerelds. Nonetheless, the reality of three daughters four years and under meant we were pretty busy. Still, it was an amazingly joyful time in our home.

Then Mom received a call that I will always remember vividly. Tom, Dad's closest friend and golf buddy, called to tell my mom that Dad was behaving very strangely. At that time, Dad was an exceptional golfer, typically scoring in the seventies or low eighties. Tom told Mom that Dad had scored in the low hundreds that day. Also, Dad seemed to have a hard time signing his scorecard. My mom had been a nurse for over twenty years at that point and had dealt with her own cancer diagnosis twenty years earlier. She was not given to overreaction when it came to physical ailments. Still, this sounded serious. It was hard not to notice the contrast between the joy of new life that God had blessed us with as Alli joined us and the somber reminder of mortality, as my dad obviously had something major going on. I helped Mom get a flight for the next day.

Mom arrived back in Tuscumbia, Alabama, and immediately took Dad in for an MRI of his brain. At first it appeared that he might have had a stroke. However, further tests revealed that cancer had metastasized into his brain. Tumors in his brain were causing him to behave as though he'd had a stroke. The original cancer was somewhere else in his body. The doctors were never able to pinpoint it conclusively, but they suspected that, since my dad had been a pretty heavy smoker earlier in life, it had originated in his lungs. My sisters and I had hoped that a mild stroke might be the wake-up call Dad needed to quit sneaking around smoking his cigars. Instead we were smacked in the head with the sobering reality that he was quite possibly going to die within a year.

Mom asked her beloved husband, "So, what do you want to do with the last little bit of time you have?"

Amazingly, Dad said, "I want to go coach these kids." Dad had just become the new head coach at Belmont High School in tiny Belmont, Mississippi, about a forty-five minute drive from his home in Tuscumbia. Dad's life was in line with his values. He loved my mom and wanted to spend time with her. He made that a priority and did it. He really enjoyed spending time with his children and grandchildren when it was possible. Most of us didn't live very close to Mom and Dad at the time, so we would travel to see him. The other priority that he continued to live out was his relationship with God and with his church family. He also continued to share with others how God had blessed his life.

So many of us want to know that at the end of our life God will be pleased with what we did. I think, in that regard, my dad lived an amazing life. When asked how he wanted to spend his last days, he said, "I want to keep doing what I've been doing." Ending our life well comes back to *living our life well*. This week, let's ask God to show us what He wants us to be doing. Let's pray that if it's what we're doing now, He would show us that He is at work in it. If not, let's pray that we would realize that we are settling for less than the best life He has for us.

TO GO DEEPER THIS WEEK . . .

» Read Jeremiah 29:10-14.
» Read 2 Timothy 4:6-8.

1. How can God be glorified through the work you are doing now, whether it is your career or schooling?
2. God has plans for all of us. What are some dream jobs or ideas you believe God could be leading you to do? What are your next steps?

Being a Great Teammate

*Supplement your faith with a generous provision of
moral excellence, and moral excellence with knowledge,
and knowledge with self-control, and self-control
with patient endurance, and patient endurance with
godliness, and godliness with brotherly affection,
and brotherly affection with love for everyone.*

2 PETER 1:5-7

Dad always emphasized to his players the importance of trust and love for their teammates. He explained that trust is earned. Teammates know what you do at practice. They know your attitude about work. They know if you're on time to meetings. They know if you are doing the little things that can make the difference between success and failure as a team. Over time, a player learns whether a teammate is truly committed to the team and therefore worthy of trust. On nearly every offensive play, for example, if someone misses a block, the results can be devastating for the ballcarrier. I specifically remember knowing that I had to trust my teammates on the Trap play. Depending on which side we ran the ball, I had to know that our guards, Lew Sample on one side and

Bernard Jackson on the other side, were going to get where they were supposed to be, or the backside defensive tackle was going to "blow me up." Lew and Bernard never let me down.

Love is a different matter. Love is a decision. True, unconditional love requires one person to put another ahead of himself. Dad would argue that knowing God was a prerequisite for truly loving anyone unconditionally. While Webster's defines *love* in terms of feelings ("tender, passionate affection"; "warm personal attachment"), the Bible defines it in terms of actions—how you treat another person. Basically, to love someone biblically is to put that person before yourself.

First Corinthians 13:4-7 gives us a biblical definition of love:

> Love is patient and kind. Love is not jealous or boastful or proud or rude. It does not demand its own way. It is not irritable, and it keeps no record of being wronged. It does not rejoice about injustice but rejoices whenever the truth wins out. Love never gives up, never loses faith, is always hopeful, and endures through every circumstance.

Football is a game that requires teamwork. On every play, eleven individuals must lose themselves for the identity of the team. Sure, some players get more individual recognition on certain plays. Still, for the *team* to work properly, the individuals must place their teammates and the overall team objectives above self. *Eleven* men giving themselves up every play of the game—it's a beautiful thing to watch. It is also oftentimes very apparent when this isn't happening. If a team is made up of people who are in it for themselves, the results are inevitably suboptimal.

In the business world, or *any* organization, even families, there is often the need for teamwork. Whatever the situation, the requirements for being a great teammate are the same. Love and trust are vital.

The apostle Peter spoke to the early church about growing in faith and character, and about how this would ultimately prove that their faith was true. In the verses quoted at the beginning of today's reading, he actually uses two different Greek words to describe different kinds of love. The word *phileo* is translated "brotherly affection" and refers to the love you feel for your good friends. The other kind of love described in the New Testament is called *agape* love. This kind of love should be like God's love: unconditional, sacrificial, impartial, not expecting anything in return.

This week, let's ask our Father to make us great teammates. Whether at work, on a sports team, or in our homes, let us seek to be people who are worthy of trust and who are growing in our ability to love as brothers and sisters, *and* as our Father loves.

TO GO DEEPER THIS WEEK . . .
» Read 2 Peter 1:1-10.

1. Are there ever circumstances in which it is *hard* to be a good teammate? What are these situations? Why do you think it is difficult?

2. What are some "teams" you are a part of now? Name them (family, work, etc.). What roles do you serve on these teams? How can you be a great teammate in these roles?

PART 3

"Like the football player who has the end zone
in his sights, as men designed in the image of God,
we were born with purpose. We are meant to live in light
of that purpose. We were designed to win."

Honor Women

You husbands must give honor to your wives. Treat
your wife with understanding as you live together.
She may be weaker than you are, but she is your
equal partner in God's gift of new life. Treat her as
you should so your prayers will not be hindered.

1 PETER 3:7

Growing up the middle child between two sisters was an adventure. (God was apparently preparing me for my life as the father of four daughters!) Early in my childhood, my dad began to teach me about how to treat girls and women. He made it very clear that they were to be treated with honor and respect. He taught me that I should always open doors for them. He taught me how to pull a chair out for them at the dinner table. He explained that I should walk on the outside of a sidewalk if walking with a woman. (This was apparently taught to young men in the days of dirt roads in order to protect the women's clothing from mud spatters.)

Today, I am very close to my sisters, Jessica and Jill. We were close as kids, too, but that definitely didn't stop us from having some rough moments. Like most kids, we occasionally had arguments. I can remember my older sister clocking me once with a closed-fist punch to the eye. Another time she pushed me accidentally, making me trip and hit my head on a table. The resulting injury required multiple stitches. (To be fair, she wasn't trying to injure me. That time.) I'd love to say that, in keeping with my dad's instruction, I never retaliated against my sisters. But I can't. (Especially after that punch to the eye. I believe I attempted a karate kick to the belly in response.) I can say that those were incidents that I hoped Dad didn't hear about. He was adamant that I never touch my sisters or any other female in a way that could cause them harm. More than that, my father demanded that I speak to women, especially my mother, with the utmost respect.

As I have grown older, Dad's wisdom regarding how to treat the "fairer sex" has benefited me. In a day when so many boys and grown males (notice I didn't call them men) treat women as objects or simply don't show them respect, I'm glad my dad taught me the truth about how to treat women.

The Bible has a lot to say about this topic. It shows high regard for the various roles that women have played throughout history and portrays many women as heroes of the faith. Right off the bat in Genesis, God teaches us that even with a vibrant relationship with Him, man still longed for the perfect physical companion. God, as the Loving Father, gave us woman to be our ideal helper and companion. As we read the New Testament accounts of Jesus' life, we learn of Mary's faithfulness and obedience in conceiving, bearing, and raising Him. Several other women are mentioned prominently in the New Testament. Jesus was very close to Mary and Martha, the sisters of Lazarus. He approached and showed respect to a Samaritan woman at a well in a remarkable story of redemption. Paul references several women who were used greatly by God in the early church—Euodia, Syntyche, Phoebe, and Priscilla, to name a few.

Still, God makes it clear in Scripture that women are different from men and that men and women have differing roles. The verse that opens today's reading is often scrutinized and can be controversial or even offensive to some.

I believe a major reason that this verse bothers people is because of the incorrect, unbiblical teaching many have received in recent years regarding human physiology, psychology, and sexuality. The Bible in no way diminishes women. It honors them. It does, however, point out the obvious fact that men are generally physically stronger than women. God speaks to us through the Bible and commands us that as men, rather than exploiting our physical strength to dominate our wives, we are to honor them as our equals.

This week, let's ask God to make us good husbands,

sons, and brothers. If you are married, ask that you would love your wife as Christ loved the church and gave Himself up for her. Ask Him to help you love all the women in your life in a way that honors God.

TO GO DEEPER THIS WEEK . . .
» Read Ephesians 5:25-28.

1. As a married man, I've emphasized the role of husbands in this entry. Read 1 Timothy 5 for more on relating to a woman who is not your wife. What do you think are some reasons for so much disrespect toward women in our culture at times (domestic violence, objectifying language, etc.)?
2. What are some ways you can "give yourself up" for your wife? If you aren't married, what are some ways you can show honor to women this week?

Avoid Negative Plays

Promote the kind of living that reflects wholesome
teaching. Teach the older men to exercise self-control,
to be worthy of respect, and to live wisely.

TITUS 2:1-2

My dad always exhorted his teams to avoid negative plays. By negative plays he didn't mean plays on which the team gains very few yards or even loses yardage, though he obviously preferred big gains or touchdowns on every play. But when Dad said, "Avoid negative plays," he meant avoid self-inflicted disasters. Fumbles and interceptions are definitely negative plays, but turnovers are their own category of bad. Usually a negative play comes from a player (or players) making poor decisions. When a running back reverses field multiple times, giving ground each time, it may result in a major negative play if he is tackled while continuing his regressive weave. A quarterback who has dropped back to pass may have a hard time finding an open receiver. He can take off and run for positive yards, or he may throw the ball away (out of bounds). Neither of those are negative plays. Continuing to look downfield, possibly drifting back from the line of scrimmage, only to be sacked—that's a negative play.

Similarly, it's important to avoid negative plays in our work and relationships. As in football, there may be times when progress seems slow, or when you even feel that you're going backward. Situations and circumstances occur that are out of our control. As we talked about earlier, we are to do our best and seek to "fall forward" in times like these—recognize the problem and make the best of it. Negative plays in life occur when we make decisions that aggravate an already difficult circumstance.

An area that often seems to fool people into making negative plays is the realm of finances. A small debt becomes a larger one as we make poor decision after poor decision, like a running back who thinks if he reverses field enough times the circumstance will change, only to find out that he has lost twenty-five yards. Many of us get impatient with our circumstances and allow ourselves to make decisions out of line with God's plans for us.

In 1 Samuel we read about the new king of Israel. Young Saul was eager. He wanted to win. He wanted to succeed. However, Saul's circumstances weren't looking good. He was facing an enemy, the Philistines, who far outnumbered his men. They seemed to have outflanked him as well. Many of Saul's men were frightened, and some were fleeing or hiding. Not the best situation for the young king. Saul had been instructed by the prophet Samuel to wait for him to come and offer the sacrifices. On the day Samuel was supposed to arrive, Saul got anxious as the hours passed and the prophet didn't show up. So Saul decided to offer the sacrifice himself. As Saul was finishing, Samuel arrived. Samuel told Saul that he would lose his kingdom as the consequence of his disobedience.

In this passage it is clear that God had a way out for Saul even though circumstances didn't look good, but Saul was too impatient to take it. Negative plays in life, like negative plays in football, generally occur when we make independent, impatient decisions to do our own thing rather than what we know we should do.

The remedy for negative plays in our lives is to walk in the power of the Holy Spirit. This week, let's ask God to change us from the inside out. Let's ask Him to help us make our decisions under the power and influence of His Spirit. Let's ask our Father to give us patience and trust in Him that He will work in whatever situations we face.

TO GO DEEPER THIS WEEK . . .
» Read 1 Samuel 13:1-14.
» Read Galatians 5:22.
» Read James 5:7-8.

1. Can you think of a time when you struggled to be patient? Describe it. What did you do? How did it turn out?
2. Why do you think we get so impatient at times? Ask God to show you the root of your impatience and to help you to turn from it and to trust Him.

Keep Your Feet Moving!

Don't you realize that in a race everyone runs, but
only one person gets the prize? So run to win!

1 CORINTHIANS 9:24

One of the earliest things I can remember my dad and other coaches teaching me and my teammates was to keep our feet moving. Whether you were a lineman, back, receiver, or linebacker, when contact was initiated, the coaches wanted your feet to keep moving.

In junior high I played quarterback on a team that ran the Wishbone offense. The Wishbone is what is known as a full-house backfield. A full-house backfield features all the backs—quarterback, fullback, and two halfbacks—all lined up directly behind the center. The fullback is about three yards directly behind the quarterback. The two halfbacks are about a yard behind the fullback, one on the left and one on the right. With all the backs in the back-field, the passing options are limited. There are only two eligible receivers who aren't lined up directly behind the quarterback. So to say that my junior high team was almost exclusively a running offense would be an understatement. The primary play in the Wishbone offense is known as the Triple Option. On that one play—depending on how the defense responds—either the fullback, quarterback, or halfback may end up with the ball! But no matter who is carrying the ball, they need to keep their feet moving if they are going to have a chance to score.

Sometimes, rather than keeping his feet moving, a player will dig in to keep from getting moved backwards. I've seen it, and I've done it. I think that some part of us instinctively thinks that digging our feet in will allow us to withstand the defense's effort to stop us. The problem with that strategy is that once you dig in, all forward motion has stopped. Even if the defense doesn't bring you down, the best thing that will happen is you'll stay right where you are. Worse, you become a stationary target. Defenders can come in and deliver brutal hits all over your body. You're a sitting duck. But when your feet are moving, even if you are getting pushed back, sometimes it causes the defender's hands to slip off of you. As your legs churn, defenders who may have dug in when they hit you start to fall away. Because your feet are moving, you begin to gain momentum, until finally you have *broken all the tackles*! At that point, you are running free with a chance to score.

In life, I've seen the same thing to be true. You really

can't dig in and expect to move forward. In relationships, in business, even in our hobbies, if we aren't *growing*, we stagnate and stop making progress. As living creatures, we are designed to grow. We are also designed with purpose. Like the football player who has the end zone in his sights, as people designed in the image of God, we were born with purpose. We are meant to live in light of that purpose. We were designed to *win*.

You may have heard the old adage "Idle hands are the devil's workshop." Second Thessalonians 3:6-13 and 1 Timothy 5:11-13 indicate that Paul knew idleness could lead to sinful behaviors. Scripture is full of references that we are to keep moving forward. Becoming a Christian isn't the end of the journey.

This week, let's look for ways that we can keep our feet moving. Let's ask God to show us ways we can grow in our relationship with Him and move from learning *about* Him to actually *knowing* Him and *experiencing* Him in our lives.

TO GO DEEPER THIS WEEK...
» Read 1 Corinthians 9:24-27.
» Read Colossians 2:6-7.
» Read 2 Thessalonians 3:6-13.

1. What are some things you can do to move forward in your Christian life?

2. What is the difference between knowing *about* God and *knowing* God? Ask God to help you grow in heart knowledge as you grow in head knowledge.

Ignorant versus Stupid

Fear of the LORD is the foundation of true knowledge,
but fools despise wisdom and discipline.

PROVERBS 1:7

If he were starting his career today, my dad may not have become the successful coach and teacher that he was. Dad was known for telling it like he saw it—there was very little political correctness in his life. He didn't think he was doing any favors to people by sugarcoating things. He wanted to help people live in the real world.

Dad made a strong distinction between ignorance and stupidity. He didn't really attach IQ to either. Sometimes a person with a really high IQ can be very stupid. Dad defined stupidity as having been given every opportunity to know the truth, but refusing to hear it. Ignorance, on the other hand, is simply a lack of exposure to knowledge. There is no shame in ignorance as long as a person is willing to learn. We all come into the world ignorant of everything outside of our immediate experience.

Dad used to teach science and history. The day before tests, he would give an exhaustive review of *everything* that was going to be on the exam. He would literally have the test in front of him while going through all the material that had been covered. Even so, some students chose not to pay attention to the review, and as a result they did poorly on the test. Dad was always frustrated when he took the time to give his students every opportunity to succeed and some just didn't want to.

We live in a day when it seems that many in the world around us either don't care to actively pursue the truth, or don't *want* to know the truth even when it is presented. For many people, this desire to avoid the truth is rooted in their desire to avoid submitting to *any* authority outside of themselves. This is an avoidance of ultimate truth—that is, the existence and supremacy of God. Those of us who have made a decision to follow Christ may still succumb to a desire to avoid truth in areas that may seem to be of less significance. We can be stubborn with dogmatic views and opinions and our desire to be "right." The root of both situations is the same. That root is pride, and it causes us to miss God.

The Bible is full of warnings about pride. What we find in these verses is that pride sets people up for failure, but fear of the Lord brings knowledge and wisdom.

In the book of Romans, we read that God makes Himself evident through creation. Some choose to ignore what has been revealed through nature. We read that they "suppress the truth" and "claiming to be wise, they instead [become] utter fools" (Romans 1:18, 22).

To fear God, we must believe in Him. As we learn to fear God, He will give us wisdom and true knowledge. Jesus desires that we know the truth. In fact, Jesus tells us that as we follow Him, we will know the truth (John 15:14-15; John 14:15-17; Matthew 7:24-27). Proverbs tells us that in the fear of the Lord we begin to have knowledge and wisdom. This week, let's ask God to help us grow in appropriate fear for Him and His power and holiness. Let's ask Him to cleanse us of pride that would cause us to suppress the truth and instead give us hearts to obey Him, that we will *know* the truth and enjoy the freedom He gives as a result.

TO GO DEEPER THIS WEEK . . .
» Read Proverbs 2:5.
» Read Proverbs 9:10.
» Read Proverbs 10:27.
» Read John 8:31-32.
» Read Romans 1:18-23.

1. Why do you think there is so much emphasis on pride in the Bible?
2. What are some areas in which you may struggle with pride? Ask God to show them to you and to help you turn from them and humbly submit to Him.

Do Your Best, and Let the Results Take Care of Themselves

To those who use well what they are given, even more will be given, and they will have an abundance.

MATTHEW 25:29

I can remember Dad telling me, "Some of the same people slapping you on the back when you're winning may be the people asking for you to be fired if you don't *keep* winning." I remember thinking to myself that, although I believed it to be true, it was still cynical to say such a thing out loud! Dad was never one to gloss over a situation. And there were expectations that he would win football games. But if you listened to Dad's day-to-day conversations and convictions about his job, you'd find that winning really wasn't what he was focused on.

Dad's focus, what he drilled into his players, was on *how we were executing*. Dad wasn't alone in this focus on execution and preparation as opposed to winning.

Legendary basketball coach John Wooden, known as the Wizard of Westwood, won ten national championships in twelve years while coaching at UCLA. The level of success, as defined by number of wins, that Coach Wooden achieved is astonishing. But this is what he said about his focus: "I felt that if [the players] were fully prepared, we would do just fine. If we won, great—frosting on the cake. But at no time did I consider winning to be the cake. Winning has always been the frosting that made the cake a little tastier."

Dad told his teams, "Whatever happens, if you give it all you've got, you should leave the field with your head held high." There was no shame in getting beaten if your preparation and effort were your best.

I have found that this philosophy is wise in life outside of athletic competition as well. Having worked in sales for roughly a quarter of a century, I am all too familiar with the pressure of winning as it pertains to where I am on the corporate scoreboard. Still, I have found that a focus on the scoreboard does nothing to help me win. It isn't a focus on the results themselves that moves me toward my objective. No, it is always my preparation, and a focus on improving myself in my skills, knowledge, and character, that moves me toward my goals.

For this week, I'd like to look back at a few of the verses from some of the previous life lesson stories:

1. Luke 16:10—The Little Things Matter
2. Colossians 3:23—Outwork Your Opponent, and Two Whistles
3. Proverbs 22:29 and Daniel 6—Better Plays Don't Win Football Games
4. 1 Corinthians 9:24—Keep Your Feet Moving!
5. Matthew 25:14-30—Characteristics of a Winner

In each of these passages, an obsession with the end result is *not* one of the critical factors that contributes to success. Each has to do with character. Luke 16:10 speaks of being faithful in the small things, which reveals that we'll be faithful in the big ones. Colossians 3:23 speaks of doing whatever we do with all our might, as it is God we are serving and not men. Proverbs 22:29 and Daniel 6 speak of the importance of excellence in giving us a platform to glorify God. First Corinthians 9:24 speaks about *how* we run the race: God tells us to run to win. Finally, in Matthew 25:14-30, we read the story of the workers that the landowner left with varying amounts of money. This story lets us know that we are to get everything we can out of the talents we've been given.

This week, let's ask God to empower us to be people of excellence and character. Let's ask Him to use our gifts and abilities as a platform to bring Him honor and praise.

TO GO DEEPER THIS WEEK...

» Review Luke 16:10; Colossians 3:23; Proverbs 22:29; Daniel 6; 1 Corinthians 9:24; and Matthew 25:14-30.

1. How can focusing on winning be detrimental to a team or individual?
2. Why do you think we sometimes become obsessed with winning?

Blue Chalk

My life is worth nothing to me unless I use it for finishing
the work assigned me by the Lord Jesus.

ACTS 20:24

When my dad was diagnosed with cancer, I flew down from Pennsylvania to be with him for his first radiation treatments, which we hoped would reduce the impact of the "mets" (metastases) in his brain. Mets are tumors that may be distant from a patient's originating cancer. The brain mets were greatly affecting Dad as they impacted his thinking and overall brain function. Reducing them would allow him to live more normally. Because of the potential effects of the tumors in his brain, Dad's doctors told him to stop driving. That meant that Mom and I would be driving him wherever he needed to go.

As I mentioned before, Dad had just taken a new position as head football coach at Belmont High School in

Belmont, Mississippi. He had a team full of kids who were hard workers but who hadn't had a lot of success on the football field. The Belmont Cardinals football team hadn't been to the play-offs in around a quarter of a century.

Dad's first radiation treatment happened to coincide with the first day of practice. The doctor and his staff took him in and, after reviewing the scans, drew lines and circles over large portions of his face with blue chalk. These blue chalk lines served as markers and targets for the medical team to aim the beams of radiation into his brain. By targeting precisely, they could limit the exposure of healthy tissue while zapping the tumors. Dad emerged from the treatment area still sporting his blue chalk lines. I asked him how he was, and he said, "Fine. You ready to go to practice with me?" I was a little surprised at his nonchalant demeanor, but I answered, "Sure. Yes, sir. Let's go!" I proceeded to drive him the forty-six miles to Belmont High School.

As we prepared for practice in the locker room, I realized that Dad still had the blue chalk lines on his face. They stayed visible throughout the practice. The other coaches and I explained to the players what the marks were and what Dad would be going through over the coming weeks and months.

The team took Dad's commitment to them to heart. *Here is a man who is having radiation beams shot through his head in the morning, and coming out into the heat of the Mississippi afternoon because he wants to coach* us! Dad's determination and commitment was reflected by his players. As he went through chemotherapy and other treatments, Dad lost his hair. His team decided to shave their heads to show solidarity with their devoted coach. As Dad's strength waned, the local townspeople bought him a golf cart to help him get around practice better. And the Cardinals were winning some football games! Sure enough, these young men had bonded and developed and finished the season by making it to the play-offs, where they lost in the opening round, 22–19 to Mound Bayou. Two months later, Coach Gerelds passed away at his home in Tuscumbia, Alabama.

In the book of Acts, Paul decided to go to Jerusalem, where he was sure to face adversity. But Paul had a firm conviction that God was leading him there. His only aim was to finish the race God had given him.

My dad was a football coach. He felt that was God's call on his life. His devotion to his players and his unabashed sharing of his faith with them made an impact on the lives of hundreds of fifteen- to eighteen-year-olds.

Whatever situation you find yourself in today, God intends to use you there. Even if you are in school or in a temporary job, *you are there for a purpose*. Remember that, really, *all* jobs are temporary.

This week, let's ask God to help us see His purposes in whatever roles we have. Let's ask Him to help us run the race He has set before us. Let's ask Him to have an impact in and through us, whatever we do and wherever we are.

TO GO DEEPER THIS WEEK . . .
» Read Acts 20:13-38.

1. Who are the people God has placed in your daily life at this time? How can God use you to have an impact on them?
2. Why do you think we often are looking forward to the "next big thing" (e.g., graduation, new job, marriage, etc.)? Ask God to help you be "all here" in the place He has you now. Ask Him to show you how you can have an impact.

Yes, Ma'am; No, Sir

Obey your spiritual leaders, and do what they say. Their work is to watch over your souls, and they are accountable to God. Give them reason to do this with joy and not with sorrow. That would certainly not be for your benefit.

HEBREWS 13:17

My wife, my two daughters (ages three and four), and I were eating at a restaurant near our home in Perkasie, Pennsylvania. When one of my daughters answered my question with "Yeah," I instructed her to say, "Yes, sir."

Suddenly, from a table behind me, I heard someone asking, "Are you in the military?" I was surprised, as I didn't think I looked very soldierly. "No. Why do you ask?" The woman replied that she had heard me instructing my daughter to say "Yes, sir" and just figured I was military. I told her that I wasn't in the military, but I had been raised by a man who believed that children should show adults respect. He taught my sisters and me to always say "Yes, ma'am," "No, ma'am," "Yes, sir," and

"No, sir" to adults. At different times during my girls' growing up, I've encountered situations when adults told my children that they didn't need to speak to them in such a respectful manner. I remember asking one of the adults about it. She said that she felt like it diminished the child. I don't know if my jaw made a sound when it hit the floor, but I'm pretty sure she recognized that I didn't agree with her assessment.

Overall, respect for others seems to be on the wane in our culture. I think respect for authority and for adults has definitely diminished in recent years. I think part of the problem may be that, as adults, we have bought into values that have elevated the place of children in our society. I know that I have been guilty of this in my own family. I can't imagine my parents giving in to my demands the way I have with my own children at times. When I was a little boy I was taught the old adage, "Children are to be seen and not heard." I'm not sure that I want to go that far in raising my children. But I don't believe that I'm doing my own children any favors by pandering to them. The real world requires that you learn to submit to authority or pay the consequences. Showing respect, whether it is to a police officer, teacher, boss, parent, or coach, is one simple way to demonstrate a submissive attitude toward those whom God has placed in positions of authority in our lives.

As opposed to diminishing those showing submission,

God's intent for authority is generally for the protection of the people in their realm (see Romans 13:1-7). Today's verse instructs us regarding those who are our spiritual leaders.

As we discussed in week 22, "Follow Your Blocks," God designed us to follow our Leader: Him. He tells us He is the Good Shepherd and we are His sheep. He has ordained others in our lives to take roles of leadership as well. As we learn to submit to others, we will be better able to submit to our Father in Heaven. The Bible makes it clear that there are times when human leadership may be unjust, harmful, and wrong, but we are to submit to God above all (see Acts 5:29).

Even so, the bulk of Scripture teaches us submission to and respect for those in authority over us. This week, let's ask God to give us submissive hearts to those whom God has appointed as our authorities, that we may, by our behavior, have opportunity to bring honor to Christ. Let's ask Him to help us learn to trust Him and submit ourselves completely to His leading in our lives. For those of us in leadership roles, whether at work or at home with our families, let's ask God to help us to be godly leaders and to look out for those under our care.

TO GO DEEPER THIS WEEK . . .
» Read Acts 5:17-42.
» Read Romans 13:1-7.

» Read Titus 3:1.
» Read 1 Peter 2:13-15.

1. What are some characteristics of great leaders?
2. Who do you think of when you list those characteristics? Who are the best leaders you have known in your life?

Your "Want-To"

Consider it a sheer gift, friends, when tests and challenges come at you from all sides. You know that under pressure, your faith-life is forced into the open and shows its true colors. So don't try to get out of anything prematurely. Let it do its work so you become mature and well-developed, not deficient in any way.

JAMES 1:2-4, MSG

One season, Dad's team came into the year with a tailback who was being recruited by several schools. He'd even been mentioned in some of the national magazines as a top recruit. Watching him on film, and playing with and against him at practice, I could tell that he was talented. The season opened up with two heartbreaking losses to two good teams—we lost by a combined total of three points. During those games, our talented tailback played well. He didn't do anything spectacular, but he was fairly effective. The next game out, we played a much weaker team. Now our star tailback *looked* like a star tailback. He had several long runs, one of them around eighty yards for a touchdown. *This* is what we were looking for! We won the game 25–0!

Next we traveled out to Leighton, Alabama, home of the Colbert County High School Indians. They were a perennial power with numerous state championships. They were in a higher classification than we were and truly loaded with talent. Still, we had shown that we could compete with good teams in our first two games. Many of us approached the game with hopes of knocking off this giant. But it wasn't happening. From the outset, the Indians absolutely destroyed us. Worse yet, our star tailback seemed to be dogging it. At one point early in the game, after one of Colbert County's many touchdowns, he was hit pretty hard on a kickoff return. As Dad was sending the play in to the offense, he noticed that his tailback was not in the huddle. He began looking up and down the sideline and couldn't find him. He asked the other coaches, but no one knew where he was. Finally, someone pointed him out—"He's up there, Coach." The tailback was sitting in the bleachers with his mom. My dad was totally taken aback. He eventually got his player back to the sideline, but the tailback's career was effectively over. Dad was going to give him a chance to earn his way back through completing after-practice disciplinary drills, but the player wasn't willing. He didn't have what coaches call "want-to," the willingness to do what is necessary to succeed.

Want-to is proven or exposed in the tough times. We all want to *be* successful. But there is a big difference between wanting the payday and being willing to do the work that is required for the payday. God knows this about us and encourages us to fight through.

In my own life I have gone through some particularly difficult times. There have certainly been times I wanted to go sit in the bleachers. There have undeniably been times when I didn't have the want-to to move on. Still, God is there, in the difficulty. He means to use it for our good (see Romans 8:28). If you aren't going through difficulty or trials right now, use the time to feed your soul with the truths of God's goodness and love toward you. Jesus tells us that tough times *will come* for all of us. But He also tells us that through Him, we will overcome (see John 16:33)!

This week, let's ask God to give us the want-to to persist through whatever difficulties we are dealing with or will deal with in the future. Let's ask Him to give us confidence that *He* is good and that He will use these times to make us into the people He wants us to be.

TO GO DEEPER THIS WEEK . . .

» Read John 16:33.
» Read Romans 8:28.

1. Can you think of times when you wanted to "go sit in the bleachers"? What were the feelings you had that led to that desire to give up?

2. Are there difficulties you are facing right now? How are you dealing with them? Do you have people to go to for help? Are there people you know who might be struggling right now? Can you help them?

It Ain't Complicated

The Master said, "Martha, dear Martha, you're fussing
far too much and getting yourself worked up over nothing.
One thing only is essential, and Mary has chosen it—
it's the main course, and won't be taken from her."

LUKE 10:41-42, MSG

In describing the game of football, Dad would often talk about the simplicity of the game. He stressed that *simple* shouldn't be confused with *easy*. On the contrary, football is extremely difficult. He would tell his players during summer practices, "If you don't love this, you should do something else. This is too much work, and too hard, if you don't love it." There was no doubt in his mind as to the difficulty of the game. On the other hand, he would say, "It ain't complicated." Again, I think one of the reasons the game resonates with so many people is this dichotomy of difficulty and simplicity. In all the discussions about complex offensive and defensive systems that people have developed, the game is still usually won or lost based on a few simple factors:

1. Who blocked better?
2. Who tackled better?
3. Who executed better?
4. Who made the fewest mistakes?

So the winning formula is quite simple. But it *isn't* easy. It isn't complicated. But it *is* difficult. To win the battle of the trenches, offensive linemen must spend hours learning their assignments. They must also perfect their technique, which involves hours of drills. Some of those drills will have them pushing a sled. Some may have them firing off and running through chutes that may be no more than five feet high in order to make sure they are staying low to the ground so they can get their pads under the defender's pads for leverage. That takes care of blocking. Then the linemen move over to defense and go through all that is involved in tackling better. Then they move on to execution and eliminating mistakes. A lot of hard work is involved in mastering those simple factors that usually lead to wins.

I have found the same thing to be true in nearly all of my life outside of football. No matter the complexities of the job you are doing or the classes you are taking or the relationships you are navigating, there are usually some simple truths and objectives that, when followed and implemented, lead to success. Oftentimes, these simple goals are extremely difficult to achieve. However, they remove the complexities and boil things down to the essentials: *What is really necessary for success in this endeavor?*

I feel like in my Christian life, as well, I have often overcomplicated things. In today's verse, Jesus said something similar to my dad's "It ain't complicated." In this passage it's so easy to relate to Martha. She was doing so much! She was working hard for Jesus. But Jesus made it clear that Martha was missing out on the best— *Him*! I have been the same way so often. Elsewhere in Scripture, Jesus makes it clear that obedience to Him is evidence that we are truly His followers (see John 14:15, 31; Luke 6:46).

Jesus has simplified our Christian life: sit at His feet and listen to Him and get to know Him. Obedience and service overflow out of the time you spend contemplating Him: who He is and what He has done for us. Simple. But difficult. As a matter of fact, apart from God's Spirit, it isn't possible. But, through His Spirit, all things are possible (see Matthew 19:26 and Philippians 4:13).

This week, let's take time to really sit at Jesus' feet. Let's ask God to empower us to come to a deeper knowledge of Him and what He has done for us, expanding our knowledge beyond our brains to our hearts.

TO GO DEEPER THIS WEEK . . .
» Read Matthew 19:26.
» Read Luke 6:46.

» Read John 14:15, 31.
» Read Philippians 4:13.

1. What are some things you've done in your life that were simple but difficult?
2. Why do you think it is difficult for some people to simply sit still listening to and conversing with Jesus?

There's Only One Who'll Never Let You Down

Do not be afraid or discouraged, for the LORD will personally go ahead of you. He will be with you; he will neither fail you nor abandon you.

DEUTERONOMY 31:8

My dad and I had a good relationship. I was blessed to have a father who was committed to me and our family. But because of my admiration for my dad as I was growing up, I believe that I had unrealistic expectations for him as a parent. I had a difficult time recognizing that my dad was still a sinner saved by grace who had the capacity to mess up. I can remember a conversation we had when I was in high school. Dad told me, "Son, we all mess up. People are gonna let you down. There is only One who'll never let you down." I knew he was talking about Jesus. I appreciated that conversation, but I think I wasn't old enough, and definitely not wise enough, to understand the significance of what Dad was communicating.

As I grew from a boy to a young man, the way I related

to my dad began to change. This was particularly true after I went off to college. The conversations I had with my father changed from those between a boy and a man, to more of those between two friends. I can remember riding down Sixth Street in Tuscumbia, Alabama, when Dad asked me for advice on something. It was a special moment for me as I realized that he respected my opinion. After I graduated from college, I began to deal with entering into manhood myself. I had met the woman I would marry and was now working in the real world. At this time, I began to struggle with a lot of identity issues. For the first twenty-three years of my life, I'd looked at one model of masculinity—my dad. I actually had to begin to deal with areas in my upbringing where I had felt let down by my father. I had basically set up my dad as an idol, even though he'd tried to explain to me that he hadn't done everything right. I was going to him for my significance when there is really only One to whom I should go.

Dad and I ended up having some difficult but liberating conversations. I was able to address areas where I felt he had really let me down. He was truly repentant for the hurts he'd caused. Perhaps more importantly, I had to examine my own sinful reactions to hurt, pain, and rejection. I needed to repent of my own sinful behaviors. I am reminded of a quote by John Calvin: "Man's nature, so to speak, is a perpetual factory of idols."

In my own life I was able to work through many of my

identity issues as Dad and I hashed out some of our previous experiences. But then I married my beautiful wife and found that the validation that I had sought from my father I was now seeking from my wife. Once again, I had to work through issues of identity.

God alone validates a human being! No one else is capable of doing it. As believers we have been created to *affirm* what God alone can validate. As believers, we must train ourselves to go to the only One who can give us the validation we so deeply desire. Jesus Christ lived *our* perfect life. We have *His* righteousness. Outside of Jesus, God the Father, and the Holy Spirit, everyone we seek our identity from will inevitably let us down—because we're not supposed to find our identity in them. Our identity is in Christ. Read today's verse and this week's "To Go Deeper" Scriptures to find out what God says about us. As you read the verses, keep in mind that God doesn't lie (see 1 Samuel 15:29)!

This week, let's ask God to show us where in relationships we may be looking for identity and self-worth apart from Him. Let's ask Him to help us turn from those areas and turn to Him alone to give us our identity and the validation we all desire. Let us thank Him for the many promises He gives us that He will never let us down!

TO GO DEEPER THIS WEEK . . .
» Read Deuteronomy 7:6.
» Read 1 Samuel 15:29.

» Read Psalm 17:8.
» Read Psalm 139:14.
» Read Hebrews 10:21-23.

1. Do you have relationships that you sometimes allow to define you as opposed to relying on God's opinion of you?
2. After reading the passages above, list some things God says about you and about Himself.

Building a Clock

Even fools are thought wise when they keep silent;

with their mouths shut, they seem intelligent.

PROVERBS 17:28

"Brevity is the soul of wit"—I think most of us have heard that maxim before. One of the earliest references for the quote I found was from a line in *Hamlet*. A messenger named Polonius comes to bring the king and queen a report that is in no way brief. Tucked into his meandering, somewhat nonsensical discourse, he inserts the phrase to boast about his sharp wit and the appropriate delivery of his message. What Polonius doesn't know is that his listeners think him neither witty nor brief. My dad had his own less Shakespearean phrase for people who talk too much: "If you ask him what time it is, he'll build you a clock."

When I was growing up, there was little public awareness of the neurodevelopmental disorder ADHD. If there had been, I might have been the poster child for raising awareness. There is no doubt that I was hyperactive, had a very limited attention span, and, *man*, did I love to talk. Fortunately, *most* of the time, my parents were very patient with me. Still, my dad would often rein me in. I heard from him innumerable times that "God made us with two ears and one mouth for a reason." I understood. But, boy, I really liked to talk. So even though I understood that talking too much could be a bad thing, I had a tough time learning to control myself.

As I grew older, I began to grow in self-awareness. I also started to interact with people who I determined must love to talk *even more* than me. I realized that rather than being engaging and fun, talking too much could actually be off-putting for many people. I also realized that rather than showing people that I cared about them, I might have been showing them that I really cared more about myself and what I wanted to say.

In the business world, especially in sales, I have learned that not knowing when to be quiet can lose you business. Salespeople have literally talked a customer right out of buying. Similarly, in relationships, I have found that talking too quickly or too much can lead to heartache and conflict. Whether it is in business, in relationships, on sports teams, or in any circumstance that requires human interaction, I believe Dad's reminder that we have "two ears and one mouth" is wise. Learning to be better listeners would do *everyone* some good.

The Bible actually has quite a bit to say about this subject. James wrote a lot about the impact of the tongue in his book. In James 3 we read about the power of the tongue. We also learn that in controlling our tongue we are better able to control every part of ourselves. The book of Proverbs also has quite a bit of instruction regarding our words.

This week's verse reminds me of another saying my parents taught me: "It is better to keep your mouth closed and let people think you are a fool than to open it and remove all doubt." The original source for this quote seems to be in dispute. Some people say that it was Abraham Lincoln, and others that it was Mark Twain. Regardless, Solomon, under God's inspiration, penned something just like it in Proverbs 17:28 roughly three thousand years ago. It is truth.

In Ephesians 4:29 we read: "Do not let any unwholesome talk come out of your mouths, but only what is helpful for building others up according to their needs, that it may benefit those who listen" (NIV). The beginning of the verse obviously has to do with avoiding dirty, impure, or lewd talk. However, looking at the rest of the verse, it is apparent that our mouths are to be used to uplift and benefit others around us.

This week, let's ask God to help us guard our tongues. Let's ask Him to help us to speak only in ways that benefit those with whom we interact. Let us repent of using our mouths to bring ourselves glory, and this week, let's use them to build up others and glorify our Father in Heaven.

TO GO DEEPER THIS WEEK . . .
» Read Proverbs 10:19.
» Read Proverbs 13:3.
» Read Proverbs 15:2, 28.
» Read Proverbs 18:7.
» Read Proverbs 18:21.
» Read Proverbs 21:23.
» Read James 3.

1. Can you recall a time when you became aware that you had probably said too much? What happened?
2. Have you ever been around someone who talked too much? How did that person make you feel? What are some ways you can check yourself to make sure you're not too loose with your tongue?

One Play at a Time

Don't worry about tomorrow, for tomorrow will bring
its own worries. Today's trouble is enough for today.

MATTHEW 6:34

I've talked about how Dad was obsessive about the
details of each play. He stressed that winning each play
is the key to winning the game. Those who read my book
Woodlawn or saw the movie know that my dad played
ball at Auburn University. As a result, I am an unabashed
Auburn fan. Notwithstanding that fact, I want to take
a moment to talk about a man I regard as possibly the
greatest college football coach of all time, even though
he is the head coach at the University of Alabama. At
Alabama, Coach Nick Saban has led the most remarkably
successful era in college football that I have ever witnessed.
As of this writing, Coach Saban just completed his tenth
season at Alabama. His teams at Alabama have amassed
an astonishing record of 119 wins against only 19 losses.

That is an average of nearly *twelve* wins a year. The basis for this sustained success is what Coach Saban has termed the Process. I have heard Coach refer to the Process in interviews and read more about it in Monte Burke's book *Saban: The Making of a Coach*.

Burke explains that the Process began to take shape in 1998, when Saban was coaching at Michigan State. Leading up to a big game against undefeated Ohio State, Saban's team was lacking confidence, and Saban turned to his friend Michigan State psychology professor Lionel "Lonny" Rosen for help. Rosen told the players that the average football play lasts seven seconds. He instructed them to ignore the scoreboard or end result of the game and instead focus only on winning in the next seven seconds.

The game didn't go as they planned. The Spartans fell behind 17–3 and then 24–9. Still, they were somehow able to battle back for a stunning 28–24 victory. Coach Saban said later that the key to the game was his team's ability to focus only on the next play.

The Bible teaches us that faithfulness in the small things leads to faithfulness in the big things (see Luke 16:10). In his famous Sermon on the Mount, Jesus teaches His disciples about where their focus should be as they deal with day-to-day life: "Seek the Kingdom of God above all else, and live righteously, and he will give you everything you need" (Matthew 6:33).

As we read Scripture we notice a theme: keep the main

thing the main thing. And though we are encouraged to count the cost and to plan for the future, we are exhorted not to worry, be anxious, or boast about things beyond what God has given us to deal with in the present (see Philippians 4:6; James 4:14). In the present we are to seek Him, seek to live righteously, and seek to be faithful in the little things.

This week, each morning, let's come to God with our fears, our anxiety, our worries, and even our plans. Let us offer them all up to Him. Then, let's ask Him to empower us to be faithful in what He brings into our lives each day. Let's ask Him to help us focus on one play at a time, trusting that He has already won the victory.

TO GO DEEPER THIS WEEK . . .
» Read Luke 16:10.
» Read Philippians 4:6.
» Read James 4:14.

1. In your day-to-day activities at this point in your life, what does taking it one play at a time look like? What processes are involved in your job, studies, and home life?
2. Think through the next big project, job, or event you may have coming up. Break it down into the individual steps required to complete the job. Ask God to show you how to be excellent in each step.

If They Don't Score, They Can't Win

*Put on every piece of God's armor so you will be able
to resist the enemy in the time of evil. Then after the battle
you will still be standing firm.*

EPHESIANS 6:13

My dad's team at Deshler High School set a state scoring record in 1990. This was before high schools began running the hurry-up and spread type of offenses so much, so needless to say, the record has since been broken. But at the time, running a traditional, huddling, run-based offense, Dad's team became the first in Alabama high school history to score six hundred points. Still, what people don't realize is that my dad was every bit as good of a defensive coach as he was an offensive one. That same team only allowed 160 points, or an average of 10.7 per game, and had four shutouts. Only two of fifteen opponents scored more than twenty points against that team. Those are amazing stats, and yet they are largely overlooked by many fans.

I guess we all love seeing exciting scoring plays—long

passes, great runs, explosive kick returns. Those plays, where a player's speed is on display as he races toward the end zone, *are* thrilling. Still, there's a reason people say, "Defense wins championships." Commentators, coaches, and players all know this to be true. To be sure, a good offense is important. But why would those who are most knowledgeable about the game say that *defense* wins championships? My dad's answer was simple: "If they don't score, they can't win."

These days a lot of teams get into scoring matches. There is tremendous pressure put on the offense to keep up. One mistake. One fumble. One interception. Any of these things may put a game out of reach. A great defense can relieve this pressure. A great defense may allow an offense to play with confidence. It may allow them to play loose, as some folks call it. When the pressure is on, players sometimes tighten up. Knowing that their defense can stop the other team allows coaches to make different decisions in certain situations.

Great defense, whatever the sport, comes down to knowing your opponent's strengths and vulnerabilities. You must also understand how they go about attacking *their* opponents. You study film. You look for tendencies. It's equally important to know your own strengths and vulnerabilities. *How can we leverage our strengths to best attack the opponent?* And critically important is the question, *How can we best protect our areas of weakness?*

So what does playing great defense look like in everyday life? All the principles mentioned above apply in the business world. Competing companies look for vulnerabilities in their competitors' products, services, and so on. Maximizing our strengths and mitigating our weaknesses is how we win in competitive situations.

In our family life, there are various things, some of them good, that may encroach upon our time with our families. As husbands and fathers, it is important that we defend our families from these invasions. We need to purposefully set limits for ourselves and our children to ensure we protect our family time and our family itself. My children rarely see boundaries and limits as good things. Still, God intends for parents to protect their children from others who would harm them and even to protect them from themselves. (My wife and I have often heard groans when we have made it a point to get to know our children's friends.) It's also important to speak truth to my family members. My wife and daughters need to hear from me about the strengths and gifts I see in them. Ultimately, I am to direct them toward their heavenly Father, who is their ultimate defender, protector, and provider.

For us as Christians, the principles are the same, but the fact that the battle has already been won changes the dynamics a bit. We are fighting an enemy who knows he has lost. Still, he wants to inflict as much damage as possible in the time he has left.

We know from 2 Corinthians 2:11 and Ephesians 6:11 that our enemy schemes and strategizes to try to destroy us. But Ephesians 6:13-17 also tells us that God gives us what we need to defend ourselves. These verses tell us to come to our Father with our weaknesses and allow Him to be our strength. Notice that in the list of spiritual armor in Ephesians 6, everything we are given by God is to protect us (our defense) except for His Word. His Word is our one offensive weapon. Therefore, we must learn to use it!

This week let's ask God to show us our weaknesses. Let us then ask Him for His protection in them. If you need help, like accountability of some sort, go to a fellow Christian and ask for it (see Ephesians 5:21). Don't try to ignore or hide your weaknesses. Acknowledge them to God and ask Him to help you in the battle. Ask God to teach you how to daily prepare for battle so that you will be well defended. And ask Him to teach you how to use His Word on offense.

TO GO DEEPER THIS WEEK . . .

» Read 2 Corinthians 2:11.

» Read 2 Corinthians 12:9.

» Read Ephesians 5:21.

» Read Ephesians 6:11, 13-17.

1. Why do you think we can be very hesitant to share our struggles?

2. What are some areas that you know to be a battle where you need extra help? Do you have some Bible verses to help you shore up your defense in this battle? Do you have a trusted friend or mentor you can go to for help and accountability?

PART 4

"You don't have to be the best;

you just need to be *your* best."

Born on Third Base

Because of the privilege and authority God has given me,
I give each of you this warning: Don't think you are better
than you really are. Be honest in your evaluation of yourselves,
measuring yourselves by the faith God has given us.

ROMANS 12:3

My little sister, Jill, married one of my best friends. William and I have been friends since high school. His parents are like second parents to me. They'd often find me sprawled out asleep on the floor of their den Saturday mornings following Friday night football games. Due to the regularity of this occurring and my propensity for sleeping in my underwear, they once gave me a really nice blanket as a gift. William's dad, Tom Christopher, was also a close friend of my late father. When Dad heard Tom use the phrase "born on third base," he immediately took it into his repertoire.

One day Dad and I were watching football with William and Tom. We were discussing a young coach who'd had some pretty amazing success in his first year as head coach at a major university. After that, though his team continued to win, there was evidence that maybe the foundation was eroding. The coach was doing questionable things on the field. And there were rumors (which turned out to be substantiated) that his behavior *off* the field was even more disturbing. Tom made the point that this young coach had a coaching pedigree that had opened doors for him throughout his career. The coach had also walked into a situation where the team was already loaded with future NFL players when he took over. "He was born on third base and walks around acting like he hit a triple," Tom said. There is such humorous profundity in that statement. And, my, how it rang true in that situation. But, my, how it has also reflected my own attitudes at times.

I have always been a fan of C. S. Lewis. I've read just about everything he ever wrote, and God has used his works in my life. Lewis explains in his book *Mere Christianity* that God gifts some people with really nice temperaments. These people get along with everyone. Some may think that this is a great advantage. If all there were was this world, I'd be inclined to agree. Fortunately, this world is not the end. And what may be perceived as an advantage here may not be one when we consider it from an eternal perspective. Lewis contends, and my experience confirms, that a great temperament does nothing to move us toward an eternity with God. To the contrary, for some, it may be a barrier. Lewis explains that pride is our biggest enemy. I know for certain that God blessed me with a demeanor that truly doesn't know a stranger. I didn't make myself this way. Yet there are times when I have found myself thinking, *Man, I've never met a stranger. Aren't I something?!?* Lewis explains that oftentimes our pride in our God-given talents or personality can blind us to God's goodness and *His* purposes in how He has designed us.

God knows we have a tendency to think more highly of ourselves than we ought. That's why He gave us His Word.

Growing up, Dad was always telling us, "Be grateful for what God has given you." That includes *who* He made you to be. This week, let's confess to God any areas where we have wanted to take credit for who He has made us to be. Let us thank our Father for His grace in giving us the gifts and abilities He has given us. Let us not presume upon His grace as though we hit a triple. Let us thank Him and ask Him to fully utilize us for *His* glory in whatever circumstances He brings about.

TO GO DEEPER THIS WEEK . . .

» Read Proverbs 11:2.
» Read 1 Peter 5:4-6.

1. What are some things about yourself that are obvious gifts that God has given you that may at times be a source of pride?

2. Are you using those things to glorify God? If not, ask Him to show you how!

Don't Be Defined by Your Losses *or* Your Wins

His unfailing love toward those who fear him is as great
as the height of the heavens above the earth.

PSALM 103:11

My granddad, Tommy Gerelds, was a high achiever, and he had high expectations for all five of his kids. Dad, being the eldest, was definitely expected to be successful. I think that like a lot of men, Dad spent a great deal of his childhood and early adulthood trying to make his dad proud. To be clear, there is nothing inherently wrong with desiring to make our parents proud. But this desire can turn problematic when we become dominated and controlled by it.

In 1973, my dad became a Christian. At that point he came to understand that he was loved by the God of the universe, not because of anything he'd achieved, but because he was a child of God the Father. This deep understanding of unconditional love freed my dad up to work hard, not to gain the approval of anyone on earth, but to honor his heavenly Father, and for the sake of his players. Up to this point in my dad's life, he had truly found his identity in his performance, often in athletics. When Dad became a Christian, he began to experience the freedom and joy of being loved *despite* his performance. It was during this time that he realized that his identity could be independent of his accomplishments. If Dad's team lost, that didn't define him. If they won the big game or set some sort of record, that didn't define him. Dad's desire was to allow his Father in heaven to define him.

Whether we grow up with a godly dad, an absent father, an abusive father, or a father anywhere along that continuum, we are all at risk of projecting our own perceptions of our earthly fathers onto God. Even the very best earthly father falls short of God the Father's perfection. We also bring our sin-tainted view of reality into our earthly relationships. This may subject us to expectations from others that aren't based in God's truth. Our response to these false expectations may enslave us to a performance mentality, so we are always seeking approval. This performance mind-set may manifest itself in many ways as we try to define ourselves through perceived *wins*. Some men are driven to their work, becoming workaholics. They think (often subconsciously) that if they work hard enough and achieve enough, maybe they will be worthy of love. Other men are driven to promiscuity. The conquest of a beautiful woman may make them feel worthwhile. Some are simply addicted to the approval of others, whether it be their coworkers, bosses, spouses, or children. We all need approval. The thing is, we *already have it*. The Bible teaches us that through faith in Jesus we have this approval that is the longing of our souls.

In Romans 5:8 we read that God loved us even as we were rebelling against Him. That verse tells us that even when we were complete failures with no desire to love Him back, God loved us and sent Jesus to die for us. God made it clear that you are worth everything to Him!

This week, let's ask God to show us if there are things we are doing to try to earn His approval. Let's thank Him for showing us how much He loves us through the gift of His Son. Let's also ask Him to show us any relationships, habits, or patterns where we are seeking approval in unhealthy ways. Let's ask Him to help us give those things over to Him, no longer allowing our losses *or* our victories to define us. Instead, let's allow ourselves to be defined by our heavenly Father and who He says we are.

TO GO DEEPER THIS WEEK . . .
» Read Psalm 17:8.
» Read Psalm 139.
» Read Isaiah 64:6.
» Read Romans 5:8.

1. Can you think of a time when you let a win or a loss define you? Describe it. How did it make you feel, behave, or treat others?
2. Are there losses from your past that you have continued to let the enemy use to define you? Ask God to show those things to you. Give them to Him and ask Him to show you the truth about who He says you are.

Leadership Can Be Lonely

*If you refuse to take up your cross and follow me, you
are not worthy of being mine. If you cling to your life, you will
lose it; but if you give up your life for me, you will find it.*

MATTHEW 10:38-39

"You can't make everybody happy. And you can get into trouble if that is too important to you."

When my dad took the head coaching job at Deshler High School in 1984, he had a vision for where he wanted to take the program. Getting there was going to take a lot of hard work. Dad would have to ask a lot from his players and coaches. Since he arrived in the spring, he had to get a lot done in a short time. Dad made a lot of tough decisions during that spring and summer. He definitely proved that you can't make everyone happy. In fact, it seemed at times like he couldn't make *anyone* happy. Everyone said they wanted Deshler to have a great football program. But Dad realized that *saying* they wanted a great program and *doing what was necessary* to have that program were very different things. It's easy for people to agree on things that don't cost them anything.

Dad made some decisions that were wildly unpopular that first spring. He wasn't a glutton for punishment. Like most people, he would have preferred not to ruffle feathers, to have everyone love him. But the accomplishment of his objectives won out over his desire for temporary harmony.

Dad once told me, "Leadership can be lonely." Great leaders often have to say no. They often have to make unpopular, divisive, or difficult decisions. Leaders must be grounded enough in their identity that they don't seek the approval of those entrusted to their leadership. Instead, great leaders must love those they lead enough to make an unwavering commitment to their objective. Loving those you lead requires you to be willing to say and do what is needed, even if it isn't the most popular thing at the time. Margaret Thatcher, former prime minister of Great Britain, defined *consensus* this way:

> The process of abandoning all beliefs, principles, values, and policies in search of something in which no one believes, but to which no one objects; the process of avoiding the very issues that have to be solved, merely because you cannot get agreement on the way ahead. What great cause would have been fought and won under the banner: "I stand for consensus"?

As Christians, we are called to lead. Wherever we are, whatever we are doing, we are called to lead in the greatest cause the world has ever known. As we lead, there will be times when our decisions make us the target of ridicule or rejection. Today, one of my teenage daughters was dealing with rejection from some peers because of her desire to obey God. The true mark of greatness in a leader isn't his or her popularity. Rather, it is the impact of his or her life and leadership.

Jesus Christ is the greatest leader of all time. But He said many unpopular and divisive things. In Matthew 10:37-39, Jesus tells us that anyone who follows Him must love Him more than anyone else, even our moms, our dads, or our own children! He goes on to say that we must be willing to lose our lives for Him in order to truly be found. Jesus didn't seek to win popularity contests. He knew where He was taking those who followed Him. He told them the truth, what they needed to hear. As a result, there were many who hated Him. Indeed, many came to oppose Him to the point of putting Him to death. Jesus knows what it is to be lonely in leading. Nonetheless, despite rejection, betrayal, and even physical pain and death, He has led and is leading the most amazing revolution of all time! He also tells us that as we stand for Him and lead others to Him, He will never leave us (see Matthew 28:20). We are never alone!

This week, let's ask God to help us to lead well. Let's

thank Him for the fact that He is always with us. Let us ask Him to help us when we face rejection for standing for Him and to give us strength to live in light of His purpose for our lives.

TO GO DEEPER THIS WEEK . . .
» Read Matthew 8:19-22.
» Read Matthew 10:37-39.
» Read Matthew 28:20.

1. Can you think of a time when you compromised to keep the peace instead of doing what you knew to be best? What was the result?
2. Can you think of a situation in which you did the right thing and ended up feeling rejected and alone? Describe it. What was the ultimate result?

Make Your Mistakes at Full Speed

We know that God causes everything to work together
for the good of those who love God and are called according
to his purpose for them.

ROMANS 8:28

Dad demanded excellence. He worked us and drilled us and coached us to ensure we knew what to do. Still, he knew that mistakes were going to happen. Dad was more concerned with effort. He would say, "If you make a mistake, make it going full speed!" For me, this was a kind of earthly and imperfect, yet vivid, picture of how God in His grace works in and through His children here on earth. Dad believed that good things happen when players are hustling. He taught us that even when we mess up, if we are giving it all we have, sometimes we might still make a big play. Oftentimes when watching sporting events, you may notice certain players or teams seem to get all the breaks or appear to be luckier than others. Dad believed that hard work, good preparation, and maximum effort lead to these apparent "fluke" circumstances. Dad's belief echoes the following saying, often attributed to Thomas Jefferson: "I'm a great believer in luck, and I find the harder I work, the more I have of it."

Dad saw enough football to know that sometimes a mistake may prove very costly. But he also saw enough to know that when players are giving maximum effort, they overcome their mistakes and good things happen.

My experience in life after sports has certainly validated my dad's philosophy. I have made innumerable mistakes. One that still makes me laugh happened in Molino, Florida. I had been asked to speak at Highland Baptist Church. After a couple of songs, the pastor introduced me to the congregation. I trotted up the stairs and positioned myself behind the podium. I noticed surprised looks on the faces of the congregants. I then looked over my shoulder to see the pastor standing there with a completely shocked look on his face. He had intended to give the church a preview of who the speaker would be later in the service. We still had a ways to go before I was supposed to come up. I laughed out loud and excused myself. When I came back up to speak later I faced an amused congregation eager (just not as eager as I had been!) to hear what God had put on my heart. Understanding that mistakes don't have to be terminal is extremely freeing. So is the idea that hard work and dedication may often function (along with God's hand) in turning mistakes for good.

The Bible is filled with stories of regular people who made countless mistakes but ended up being used in a major way by God. Abraham, Moses, David, Peter, Paul: they all made *major* mistakes—committed terrible sins— and yet God still used them and blessed them.

Great comfort can be found in today's verse. However, one thing it doesn't say is that all things *are* good. No. God allows bad things to happen. He allows us to mess up. But He assures us that *He* is ultimately in control and will work things for good. Another great biblical example of God overcoming a major mistake and working it for good is the story of Joseph and his cruel and unjust treatment by his brothers (Genesis 37–50). Joseph's brothers were wrong. What they did was horrible. Yet at a time in their life when only God's grace and mercy could keep them alive, He did so. And He used their own mistake to do it. Joseph's family was living through an extreme famine. Having sold their brother (Joseph) into slavery, they had no idea he was even alive. They definitely wouldn't have thought that he'd risen to power in Egypt. But, sure enough, when Joseph's brothers traveled to Egypt to seek help surviving the famine, they discovered that their brother was now able to help them or hurt them. Knowing full well how badly they had treated him, they thought he'd repay them in kind. Instead, Joseph forgave his brothers, recognizing that God used their terrible actions for good (see Genesis 50:20-21).

This week, let's thank God for His grace and mercy in

forgiving us. Let's also praise Him for the fact that He is in control. He isn't limited by our sin and mistakes. Let's ask Him for the zeal to give 100 percent effort to getting to know Him through spending time with Him in prayer and reading His Word. Then let's trust Him to work all things for good, even when we mess up.

TO GO DEEPER THIS WEEK . . .
» Read Genesis 37–50.

1. Can you think of a circumstance in which an apparent mistake turned out for good? Describe it.
2. How does knowing that God can use even our mistakes for good make you feel? Have you ever been afraid to do something for God because you were afraid you'd mess up? Don't be afraid. He's got this!

Love 'Em When You Don't Get Anything from It

The King will say, "I tell you the truth, when you
did it to one of the least of these my brothers
and sisters, you were doing it to me!"

MATTHEW 25:40

Pauline Phillips, better known as the original Abigail Van Buren of "Dear Abby" fame, once wrote, "The best index to a person's character is (a) how he treats people who can't do him any good, and (b) how he treats people who can't fight back." My dad always aligned himself with the underdog. He always wanted to give people a chance. Maybe that was because he knew what it was like to be an underdog himself.

When Dad was a junior at Woodlawn High School, he was an outstanding baseball player attracting attention from colleges and pro scouts. Even the New York Yankees were supposedly looking at him. He wasn't very big or blazing fast, but he could hit the ball, and he had a rocket arm. Then, during spring training for football, a secondary sport for him, he injured his shoulder. Badly. He suddenly went from a being a major-league prospect to being a "what could've been" story. Nonetheless, Dad was committed to playing baseball at Auburn University. He taught himself to throw the ball left-handed. During his senior season at Woodlawn, he would catch the ball, take his glove off, and throw in the ball left-handed.

After graduating from Woodlawn, Dad did go to Auburn. He bused tables in the athletes' dorm to earn money to pay for school. Dad ultimately made the Auburn baseball team as a walk-on and played a key role on Auburn's 1963 Southeastern Conference championship team.

Dad emphasized to me and my sisters that you treat people with respect *regardless* of their perceived role. My dad could be really, *really* tough at times. But he had a true soft spot for those who seemed to be on the outside looking in. I think he knew what it was like to feel as though he was being written off. He never wanted anyone to feel that way. He wanted to give everyone a chance.

Not long after finishing college, I began working in the world of sales. Many people have a bad perception of salespeople. I can understand that. However, my experience with *good* salespeople has revealed to me that some of the generalizations are simply wrong. Many of the best people I know are salespeople.

Dad taught me that all people are important. It doesn't matter whether they can benefit me or not. In my roles in sales, I often come in contact with people who aren't necessarily the ones I need to speak with regarding a purchasing decision. Still, I have a choice as to whether I will seek to be a blessing to those people or just blow past them as I pursue my sales objectives. For me, part of the fun of my job is meeting and interacting with whoever comes across my path. Many astute companies have begun to implement a tactic they call the "total office call." This tactic is simply employing the attitude that everyone in an office has value and may actually assist the salesperson in reaching his or her sales objective.

As followers of Christ, this should be our standard operating procedure. We should make it our goal to be light to everyone with whom we interact during our workday. Remembering people's names, thanking them, smiling . . . these are simple things that may be a difference maker for the people you see this week.

We read in John 13:34-35 that our love for others is often what will reveal the truth of who Jesus is to those searching for answers.

God doesn't make any mistakes. If a person lives and breathes on this earth, they are important. They have a role in God's redemptive story. This week, let's ask God to give us a heart for those who may have been left out or marginalized. Let's ask Him to give us eyes to see those around us who may have no friends. Let's ask Him to give us grace and wisdom to know how we might approach these people and *truly* love them, as He has loved us.

TO GO DEEPER THIS WEEK...
» Read John 13:34-35.

1. Who are some people you interact with whom you may be able to encourage?
2. Are there any groups in your city or town or school that you believe God is calling you to love? How might you go about doing this? Would you need to enlist the help of others? Your church? Think about it. Ask God to show you what to do.

That Ball Takes Funny Bounces

He gives his sunlight to both the evil and the good,

and he sends rain on the just and the unjust alike.

MATTHEW 5:45

I was never a very good basketball player. Still, I played a lot of pickup basketball with my buddies over the years. I prided myself on making good passes to my teammates. (That's my way of saying I wasn't a very good shooter.) I could bring the ball up the floor and did a decent job dribbling and protecting the ball so that I didn't turn it over. My ability to dribble the ball up the court with some semblance of control is due to the spherical nature of a basketball. Footballs don't share that shape.

As opposed to a sphere, a football is a spheroid. Imagine trying to dribble a football up the court. My dad used to say, "A football is shaped funny. It's not like a basketball. A football can take some funny bounces." Dad would say this in the context of strange things happening on the football field. He wanted his players to be prepared for anything. He knew that seemingly impossible things can happen in games. An example of this occurred on September 19, 2015, during a University of Alabama versus Ole Miss football game. With about thirteen minutes left in the third quarter, Ole Miss lined up for a third and short play. An errant snap started to sail over quarterback Chad Kelly's head. The ball hit his hand and bounced straight up in the air. He was able to catch it and almost simultaneously throw it up for grabs into double coverage downfield as he was being slammed to the turf by two charging Alabama defensive linemen. The ball was thrown without much velocity and was kind of fluttering out to the left flats (about five yards beyond the line of scrimmage). Wide receiver LaQuon Treadwell went up for the ball as two Alabama defensive backs converged on him. The ball actually hit defensive back Minkah Fitzpatrick's helmet and again bounced high in the air, arcing down into the waiting hands of Ole Miss wide receiver Quincy Abeboyejo, who continued on to complete a bizarre 66-yard touchdown play for Ole Miss. Not exactly the kind of play you can game-plan for, but it happened.

There are so many times in life when crazy things happen. Sometimes we are blessed with seemingly miraculous good fortune. I'm sure that the Ole Miss players were thrilled with the very fortunate bounces the ball took on that play. At other times in our lives it may seem that all the breaks are going against us. I'm sure the Alabama players could not believe that the ball bounced so perfectly

Ole Miss's way during that play. One of our challenges as believers is to trust in God's goodness in the good times *and* the bad times. I think it is tempting to either think that we have done something good to warrant God's blessings or assume we are being punished when bad things happen in our lives. In this week's verse, Jesus discusses God's ultimate control over human circumstances.

The Bible is full of stories in which God's goodness is shown in surprising ways. Jesus helped the wedding party in Cana when they were out of wine by changing water into wine. During the Exodus, God did a number of amazing things to show both the Egyptians and the Israelites that He was going to take care of His people— from bringing about plagues and signs in dealing with Pharaoh, to dividing the Red Sea for the Jews to go across on dry land while allowing it to come back together on the Egyptians. God continued to show His care and control to the Hebrew nation as He led them with a pillar of cloud by day and of fire by night. He provided them with daily bread in the form of manna from heaven as well as quail to eat and water to drink. In these circumstances we see that God is able to bring surprising blessing, nourishment, and obvious goodness into our lives. But what about when bad things happen? God's Word tells us about this, too. Job experienced horrific circumstances in his life, including the loss of his children, his wealth, and his health. As Job's misfortune mounted, his wife told him he should just curse God and be done with it. Job responded, "Should we accept only good things from the hand of God and never anything bad?" (Job 2:10).

Life is more like a football than a basketball. It bounces unpredictably. Our stability has to come from our knowledge that God is good. God is gracious. And God is in control. This week, let's praise God for His goodness, mercy, and grace, and for the fact that He is in control. Let's ask Him to help us accept whatever circumstances come our way in submission to Him. Let's trust that He actually controls the way the ball bounces and He has promised He is looking out for us.

TO GO DEEPER THIS WEEK . . .

»   Read Matthew 1:1-17. Study these people's lives to see how God uses surprising means to accomplish His purposes.

»   Read Matthew 5–6.

1. Can you think of a time in your own life when you wondered why God was allowing things to happen the way they were? What was going on? How did it work out? Is it happening now?

2. What are some things we can do when we find ourselves questioning our circumstances? List some dire situations from the Bible in which God showed that He was still in control.

Look the Ball All the Way In

Keep your eyes on Jesus, who both began and finished this race
we're in. Study how he did it. Because he never lost sight of
where he was headed—that exhilarating finish in and
with God—he could put up with anything along the way:
Cross, shame, whatever. And now he's there, in the place
of honor, right alongside God.

HEBREWS 12:2, MSG

We were playing Brooks High School my senior year at Deshler High School. The play was 34-Belly Pass. I was playing fullback. On this play I was to fake like I was getting the ball through the 4 gap, between the right guard and right tackle. I was to run five yards and cut to my right, running parallel to the line of scrimmage. Our quarterback, Russ Cleveland, zipped a perfect pass out to me that hit me in the hands. Now, I had good hands. There were better receivers on the team, but generally, if the ball hit my hands, I caught it. But not this time. As the ball hit my hands, I turned my head to my left to look upfield. I was concerned about who might be coming from that direction. The old adage "He heard footsteps" applied to me in that situation. If you're not familiar with this term, it means you either heard or imagined hearing someone coming at you outside of your span of vision. I hate to admit that I looked away from the ball, as it is a cardinal sin in football.

Dad coached his backs and receivers to "look the ball all the way in, until it is tucked with one end covered by your hand and the other end against your body." In teaching his players about catching the ball in traffic, Dad would tell us, "You're going to get hit anyway, so you may as well catch the ball." Dad would go on to explain that if you lose focus on the ball, you will most likely still take the punishment and have nothing to show for it. Nonetheless, it can still be very difficult to keep your eyes on the ball and look it all the way in when there are defensive players bearing down on you!

In this situation, I didn't catch the ball, and to make matters worse, there was no one around me. I took my eyes off the ball to protect myself from a hit *that wasn't coming*. I have seen this happen so many times in football. A player turns his head upfield before tucking the ball away. As he does so, the ball tips off his hands and falls incomplete, or worse, gets tipped up in the air and is intercepted. Meanwhile, there was no one near the receiver and if he'd just focused on the football, he could have tucked it and turned upfield for a big gain. On the flip side, some of the more heroic, spectacular catches in football history are ones where the receivers *did* have defenders bearing down on them. In spite of knowing they were going to get hammered, they caught the ball and tucked it away.

In life away from sports, it's even more important for us to remain focused on our primary objective, even when life may be throwing all sorts of obstacles in our way. Some of the more heroic lives we admire are those whose circumstances would naturally have caused someone to lose track of their purpose. Instead, these heroes stayed true to their calling. A few people whose lives have inspired me are Desmond Doss, Martin Luther King Jr., Joni Eareckson Tada, Eric Liddell, Jim Elliot, and Bruce Olson. I encourage you to look these people up and read books or see movies about their lives. They are truly inspirational.

This week's verse exhorts the church to remain focused on Christ, giving Jesus as an example of someone who lived life with God's purpose as His ultimate ambition.

This week, let's make it a point to keep our eyes on Jesus. Many things in our lives will tempt us to take our eyes off the ball. Let's ask God to help us remain focused on Him. Regardless of the daily distractions that may come our way or whatever weapons the enemy may use to try to bring us down, let's ask our Father to enable us to concentrate on Him and His purposes for each moment.

TO GO DEEPER THIS WEEK . . .
» Read 1 Corinthians 2:2.
» Read Hebrews 12:1-3.

1. What are some things in life that can be distractions for you, that cause you to take your eyes off the ball of your priorities?
2. What are some practical things you can do on a daily basis to help you stay focused on what's important?

Just Do It!

Remember, it is sin to know what you ought to do
and then not do it.

JAMES 4:17

This chapter is not a tribute to Nike's famous market-
ing campaign. Rather, it's about a father's advice to
his son who often dreamed big and out loud. As a kid I had
a tendency to talk. A lot. The way I talked reminds me of
an episode of the sitcom *Seinfeld* from back in 1991. In
this particular show ("The Pony Remark"), the character
known as Kramer tells Jerry that he is going to transform
his apartment (across the hall from Jerry's) by removing all
the furniture and replacing everything with different levels
throughout. Jerry has heard lots of far-fetched boasting
over the course of their friendship and knows that Kramer
isn't going to build the levels. So Jerry and Kramer make a
friendly wager about whether it will happen. The loser has
to buy the winner a nice dinner. The conversation starts

off with Jerry's dad asking Kramer about how the levels are coming. Kramer tells them that he's decided not to do it. Jerry sarcastically feigns shock and asks when Kramer is going to pay up with the dinner. Kramer argues that since he *could* do the levels but just decided not to, the bet is off. Jerry is flabbergasted:

JERRY: We didn't bet on if you wanted to. We bet on if it would be done.
KRAMER: And it could be done.
JERRY: Well, of course it could be done! Anything could be done! But it only is done if it's done. Show me the levels! The bet is the levels.
KRAMER: But I don't want the levels!
JERRY: That's the bet!

Like a lot of little boys, I dreamed of fantastic athletic exploits. Not only did I dream about these feats, but I liked to tell my dad about how I was going to do all these things. My dad was generally patient. He would let me go on and on about the amazing things I was going to do. Finally, after hearing endless descriptions, Dad would say, "Son, instead of telling people what you are going to do, why don't you just do it?" This may seem harsh, but understand, Dad was a man of action. Words didn't do it for him. He'd been around athletics his whole life, and he'd heard lots of people talk the talk who didn't walk the walk, so to speak. Dad didn't want his son to be someone who talked a big game but then let people down. He knew that my intentions were sincere, just like Kramer's. But he also knew that wanting to do something and talking about it were very different from actually doing it.

In today's verse, James writes about the need to take action. Earlier in his letter, he says that the evidence of our faith is the action we take. James is telling us that just talking the talk without walking the walk is useless.

This week, let's ask God to make us people of action. Let's pray that God would make us *doers* of the Word and not just talkers. Remember, God accepts us because of what Jesus did, not because of anything we do. James is telling us that if we really believe this to be true it will show up in the things we do. Let's thank our Father for this amazing grace He shows us by accepting Jesus' work on our behalf. Then, let's ask Him to give us the motivation and courage to go express our faith by doing things that demonstrate that Jesus is working in and through us each day.

TO GO DEEPER THIS WEEK . . .
» Read James 2:14-26.

1. Are there areas of your life in which you tend to procrastinate? What are they? Why do you procrastinate?

2. What are some ways that you can put your faith into action in your day-to-day life this week? List them below and share them with a friend or mentor who can help keep you accountable in your quest to be a person of action.

Every Day Is a Good Day; Some Are Just Better Than Others

God takes pleasure in your pleasure! . . .
Each day is God's gift. It's all you get in exchange for the
hard work of staying alive. Make the most of each one!

ECCLESIASTES 9:7-10, MSG

After Dad became a Christian in 1973, he coached through the 1975 football season and then resigned. He went to work with his father in the insurance business. That was a big change for Dad, as his only jobs since finishing college had been in coaching. When you consider that eight years later he went back into coaching and coached all the way up until he passed away, it kind of makes you wonder why he stepped away. I think he'd gotten to a point where he wasn't enjoying coaching anymore. The reason, I believe, is that he had let his passion for it get out of balance. It wasn't that he was obsessed with winning. As I've mentioned earlier, he knew that winning was important. But since he'd begun a relationship with Jesus, his focus had become more and more about the players and about giving them the best chance to win. I saw Dad struggle with knowing when he had done enough. I think the idea of his letting his players down and their losing the game because he hadn't done enough gnawed at him. His decision to step away when he did allowed him to develop perspective. I think learning to balance work, family, and leisure, all while learning to submit to and grow in a relationship with God, never fully goes away. It didn't for Dad. But he grew in perspective, and I think that allowed him to eventually get back to the game that he loved and, more importantly, back to "the kids," as he called his players.

Working in the business world allowed my dad to see that wins and losses don't just come on the sports field. He began to understand that losing is sometimes the thing that God uses in our lives. Don't get me wrong, Dad never took losing lightly. He still expected excellence from himself in business and from himself and his players when he was coaching.

When Dad resumed coaching, he was so energized. He got into really good shape, and he was working hard and loving it. There is a scene in the movie *Chariots of Fire* that I think exemplifies my dad's demeanor and sense of purpose while coaching. In speaking to his sister about returning to China as a missionary, Eric Liddell, an aspiring Olympic track star, explains that though he'll be returning, it will be delayed until he's finished the work God has given him as a runner.

> But I've got a lot of running to do first. Jennie. Jennie, you've got to understand. I believe that God made me for a purpose. For China. But he also made me fast. And when I run I feel his pleasure. To give it up would be to hold him in contempt. You were right. It's not just fun. To win is to honor him.

God made my dad a coach. I believe that the older Dad got, the more he realized the gift he'd been given to do what he loved every day of his life. This was exemplified in his saying, "Every day is a good day. Some are just better than others." Dad felt God's pleasure in doing the job he'd been called to. His life reflected enormous gratitude to God for the gift of each day he got to live. I think that in his final season of coaching, and in getting to spend quality time with his wife, his three children, and the kids at Belmont High School, this gratitude for each day was even more profound.

The passage today's verse was taken from ends with these words: "Whatever turns up, grab it and do it. And heartily! This is your last and only chance at it, for there's neither work to do nor thoughts to think in the company of the dead, where you're most certainly headed" (Ecclesiastes 9:7-10, MSG). That may sound a bit morbid. But the reality is that our time here on earth is limited. The Bible describes our life as "but a breath" (Psalm 39:5). Knowing this to be true, let's ask God to give us grateful hearts as we live our lives this week. Let us begin each day with a conversation with God, thanking Him for the gift of that day. Let us then ask Him to help us feel His pleasure as we seek to live out His purpose for our lives.

TO GO DEEPER THIS WEEK . . .
» Read Psalm 39:4-5.

1. What do you truly love to do? What would a perfect day look like?
2. What would the perfect job look like? What are some of your natural gifts?

When They *Stop* Coaching You Is When You Need to Be Concerned

My child, don't make light of the LORD's discipline, and don't give up when he corrects you. For the LORD disciplines those he loves, and he punishes each one he accepts as his child.

HEBREWS 12:5-6

When I was in junior high, my dad was out of coaching. This was during the seven years he was in the insurance business. During those years, I played football and baseball, and I wrestled. Throughout those years I was coached by a lot of men who had a passion for working with young people—Coaches Parker, Montalto, Russo, Slayton, Lasseter, Wood, Sanders, Hulsey, Baker, and others. I was blessed to have them in my life. Still, as a thirteen- or fourteen-year-old young man, I didn't necessarily appreciate them *every day*. I can remember coming home from practice on several occasions complaining to my parents about how this coach or that coach was riding me. I should have known what would come of my grumbling. My mom and dad were big on submitting to authority. Their take was that coaches and teachers were right unless there was indisputable evidence to the contrary. I can't remember a single time in all my growing-up years that my parents took my sisters' or my side in any grievance we had with a teacher or coach. As I expressed in week 16, "No Excuses," Dad wanted me to grow up taking responsibility for my own actions.

Beyond the principle of being responsible for my own actions, Dad also wanted me to understand that good coaches (and teachers) push their players (and students). No, they don't literally, physically push the players (especially these days, or they'd be out of a job). Instead, they push their players to work harder, to concentrate more intensely, and to become the very best they can possibly be. For a kid—and for that matter, for a lot of adults—this kind of coaching can be difficult to take. I can still clearly hear my dad telling me, "When they *stop* coaching you is when you need to be concerned." He went on to explain that great coaches don't waste their time pushing players they believe can't or won't do the job. The fact that the coaches were riding me was evidence that they believed I could do better.

My experience managing and coaching sales reps for a Fortune 500 company affirmed what my dad taught me. Generally speaking, good managers push because they believe that their team members can be better than they currently are. One principle that I learned and sought to apply while coaching our team was something I learned from a book by Marcus Buckingham entitled *First, Break All the Rules*. In his book he reveals that the best managers spend the majority of their time coaching, encouraging, and correcting their *best* reps, while other managers spend the majority of their time working on their *worst* reps. This idea echoes what I learned from my dad. Good coaches are going to really get after their best players.

God is the ultimate authority. He isn't an authority *figure*. He is *the* Authority. God is also good. All the time. Our Father in heaven knows His children. The Bible tells us that He is going to stay on us when He knows that we are veering away from becoming the best person each of us was designed to be. Good coaches, teachers, managers, and parents are actually following the design established by God. God's design for humanity is modeled through the life of Christ (see 1 Peter 2:21-23).

God's design is taught through the Word of God, the Bible (see Psalms 25:8; 32:8). He entrusts us with His image as we are created in His likeness (see Genesis 1:26), then does life with us, giving us His Spirit to live within our souls (see John 14:16-18). And finally, God corrects us through discipline (see Hebrews 12:5-11).

This week, let's consider the godly model we have for coaching and training people in our lives, whether they are our children or others we've been entrusted to lead. Then, let us thank our Father for all the ways He seeks to lead us into a deeper relationship with Himself. Let's acknowledge that even His discipline is for our good. Let's thank Him that Jesus took our punishment, and if we find ourselves in a situation where we need His loving discipline, let's submit to Him, knowing He is a loving Father.

TO GO DEEPER THIS WEEK . . .

» Read Genesis 1:26.
» Read Psalms 25:8; 32:8.
» Read John 14:16-18.
» Read Hebrews 12:5-11.
» Read 1 Peter 2:21-23.

1. Who are the people God has entrusted you to lead? Are you following this biblical model in your leading?
2. Think about the differences between *punishment* and *discipline*. List them.
3. Remember that *all* God's punishment was poured out on Jesus. Discipline is for our good to direct us back to the right path.

All That Matters Is the Color of Their Jerseys

In Christ's family there can be no division into Jew and non-Jew, slave and free, male and female. Among us you are all equal. That is, we are all in a common relationship with Jesus Christ. Also, since you are Christ's family, then you are Abraham's famous "descendant," heirs according to the covenant promises.

GALATIANS 3:28-29, MSG

When Dad took the job at Deshler High School in 1984, he inherited a team that had seen a fair amount of racial tension. When I moved there, my new friends told me about a racially motivated fight that had occurred in the lunchroom the year before we arrived. Because of the history they'd experienced, many of my African American teammates were leery, wondering if the new coach would treat all the players fairly. Dad made it very clear very early on that he loved his players. *All* his players. Dad let the team know that he would play whoever *won* the positions on the field during practice. He said, "The only color that matters to me is the color of the jersey you wear." Some African American players took a risk and trusted him. Several of them became good friends of mine. Still, it took some time to build a culture of trust and equality.

I never noticed my dad displaying any sort of racial bias. I joke that prior to becoming a Christian, he may have been prejudiced against bad football players. But otherwise, he seemed to regard everyone equally. Still, it doesn't take an in-depth study of world history to see that mankind's tenure on this earth is marred by racism and prejudices all over our planet. In the United States we have the horrible legacy of slavery and mistreatment of African Americans for well over two hundred years. Even after the Civil War, segregation and discrimination were still very much a part of many regions of our country, especially the South. The Civil Rights Act of 1964 finally removed many barriers for minorities in the United States. Still, there is lingering racism and suspicion of racism that affects relationships across our country to this day.

I could probably write an entire book on this subject, as I am very passionate about it. I believe that the church has had and can continue to have a profound impact in promoting racial reconciliation and in overcoming injustices in our society. There had been a lot of progress in this area until recent years, but the enemy seeks to divide people to take the focus off of what the *real* life-and-death issue is. That issue is the eternal well-being of every man, woman, and child of every skin tone and ethnic origin. Racism isn't a black or white issue. It is a *sin* issue. Throughout human history racism and discrimination have been the result of mankind seeking to find significance by subduing and oppressing others. Very often, God has used the transforming power of His love through the church and individual Christians to overcome these atrocities.

Galatians 3:28 teaches us that in Christ, the only color that really matters is red, the color of His blood that covers our sins. In God's eyes, our outward distinctions are irrelevant. We are also taught in Scripture that true love puts others first (see Philippians 2:3-4 and John 15:13). In 1 John 4:20, we read, "If someone says, 'I love God,' but hates a fellow believer, that person is a liar; for if we don't love people we can see, how can we love God, whom we cannot see?"

God is calling us to unite! The church has a remarkable opportunity to show God's love to a world desperately needing it. I believe that we, the church, must be intentional in engaging people outside our immediate surroundings and avoid isolating ourselves ethnically, racially, or socioeconomically. We need to continue to take purposeful, missional steps to unite the church body.

This week, let's ask God to give us opportunities to love someone who may not look like us. Let's look within our own church bodies for opportunities to engage others from different backgrounds. Let us pray for our nation, that God would continue to heal wounds from our racially divided past and unite His church across all racial and ethnic differences.

TO GO DEEPER THIS WEEK . . .
» Read John 15:13.
» Read Philippians 2:3-4.

1. Are there any people groups, races, or ethnicities you have a difficult time unconditionally loving or with whom you feel uncomfortable? Ask God to show you any areas you may be unaware of.
2. Think of opportunities you may have to engage with people who come from a different background than you. Speak to others in your church about planning a project with another church, possibly across town, in another part of the country, or in a different country.

You Don't Have to Be the Best; You Just Need to Be *Your* Best

So whether you eat or drink, or whatever you do,

do it all for the glory of God.

1 CORINTHIANS 10:31

On a team of forty to eighty players you're going to have a wide range of skills. The innate athletic ability for each player is going to vary. High school athletes range from fourteen to eighteen years of age. For some young men, the difference in physical maturity from age fourteen to age eighteen is literally the difference between a boy's body and a man's body. Also, for the majority of the year a player is *not* playing football. Those seven or eight months are spent preparing to play the game. That means spending time in the weight room and on the field or track running and doing agility drills.

When a senior-to-be is bench-pressing 375 pounds and the soon-to-be sophomore is bench-pressing 135 pounds, you can understand why some kids might feel like they don't belong. Football is a sport that allows for a wide range of sizes, speeds, and strengths, as different positions have different physical demands. Even so, when you haven't grown out of your childhood frame and some of your teammates are shaving twice a day and can deadlift a house, you may sometimes doubt whether you fit in.

Dad was very fond of measuring his players, not against each other, but against their previous personal bests. Sure, he still tracked and congratulated guys who had the very best times or lifts overall. But he made it a point to encourage personal growth and achievement against your biggest challenger—yourself. Dad taught me "You don't have to be the best. But you need to be *your* best." As a player, you don't control your genetic ceiling, the limits of what you are able to do physically. What you do control is your effort. Personal effort and commitment are what allow any individual to scrape the ceiling of his or her potential.

This principle applies equally in the business world. The best teams and individual performers in the corporate realm *never* slack off on their personal development. This commitment to expanding their knowledge and skills, while maintaining an intense work ethic, ensures that despite whatever external forces or market conditions occur, these people will get everything they can out of their abilities.

Colossians 3:23 tells us that we are to work hard for the

Lord because it is Him that we serve. We read in Matthew 25:14-30 the story of the servants entrusted with different amounts of money and what was expected of each based on how much they were given. Both of these Bible passages emphasize personal excellence in whatever we do. The parable in Matthew emphasizes that not everyone has the same gifting. The expectation, nonetheless, is that you do all you can with all you've been given. In this week's verse, the apostle Paul is speaking to the Corinthian church about foods and drinks and whether they should eat them or not. In his instructions, he once again hits upon the need to do everything as if it were for the Lord.

This week, work on a personal development plan for yourself. The goal is to develop in every facet of who God made you to be. Look for ways you can improve your *vocational* skills and knowledge. Many companies have a training and development department and some even have websites with free materials or programs you can use. Next, you may want to consider a *physical* development plan. This may be implementing a cardiovascular program or weight training (or both) as well as modifying your diet. Improving your *relationships*, especially with your spouse and family, is also a crucial area. Maybe there are some marriage books, conferences, or even Sunday school classes you could look into. Maybe instituting a date night would be helpful. Finally, your *spiritual* health, your relationship with God, always needs attention. Like with any relationship, it requires work to get to know God. Spending time reading and studying the Bible is a good start. Developing the habit of memorizing Scripture is also extremely beneficial. Spending time in prayer is essential. For those to whom all this may be new, my pastor encourages starting with just five minutes of Bible reading, five minutes of prayer, and five minutes of praise, such as listening to and singing along with some worship music. God is going to complete the work He has begun in you. This week, let's ask Him to show us how we can better participate in His improvement plan for each of us.

TO GO DEEPER THIS WEEK . . .
» Read Matthew 25:14-30.
» Read Philippians 1:6.
» Read Colossians 3:23.

1. Are there areas in your life where you feel you may be on cruise control? What are they? Can you think of ways to implement a development plan for them?
2. What is an area in which you are already skilled and feel you could grow even more? Seek to develop a growth plan in this area of gifting.

There's Worse Things Than Dying

If you try to hang on to your life, you will lose it.
But if you give up your life for my sake, you will save it.
And what do you benefit if you gain the whole world
but are yourself lost or destroyed?

LUKE 9:24-25

My dad and I sat in chairs by the pool in his back-yard. In the months following his cancer diagnosis, he and I spent lots of time out there talking. There were things he wanted to talk about, but not necessarily with my mom or sisters. He loved Mom more than anyone in the world. He loved my sisters every bit as much as he loved me. But there were conversations that he only wanted to have with a man—his son, me. Rightly or wrongly, he was concerned that some things would upset Mom, Jessica, and Jill. I'm glad that we got to have those times together. The time between learning of his illness and losing him went very quickly. We only had six months, and I was living in Pennsylvania, and he was in Alabama. I came as often as I could.

One conversation that still resonates in my heart and soul was one in which he revealed some fear about his approaching death. Dad loved God and knew that God loved him. Nonetheless, like all of us, he had moments of doubt and uncertainty. I talked to Dad about death as a door into eternity. He agreed. But the difference, he said, is that for most people, that door is way off, down some really long corridor. He was standing inches from that door. His nose was nearly touching it. It was *right there*. At that point, the reality of what is beyond that door weighed heavily on his mind and heart.

Despite this admitted fear, Dad conveyed some wisdom that has been motivational for me ever since. He said, "There's worse things than dying." He went on to talk about things that would be worse than dying:

1. Living a life without knowing God.
2. Living a life without having family and others who love you.
3. Living a life without loving your family and others.
4. Living a life with no purpose or impact.

In a nutshell, Dad was saying that living life without love and purpose was worse than dying.

This reminds me of something said by a young missionary named Jim Elliot. Elliot left the United States and went to Ecuador in the early 1950s. He went with the purpose of reaching indigenous peoples with the truth of the possibility of a relationship with God through faith in Jesus. Ultimately, Elliot and four other men embarked on a mission to reach the Huaorani people. The Huaorani were known for their violence, and no Christian missionaries had ventured into their territory for centuries. After seemingly making strides in developing a positive relationship with the tribe, Elliot and his four teammates were murdered by the Huaorani. Earlier in his life, Elliot had been quoted as saying, "He is no fool who gives what he cannot keep to gain what he cannot lose." That sounds a lot like what Jesus said in today's verse.

God desires our lives to be filled with love and purpose. He tells us clearly that clinging to life and missing Him is no life at all. So this week, let's ask God to show us areas where we may be clinging to our own lives. Let's ask Him to teach us how to let go and then to empower us to do it. There are definitely worse things than dying. God wants us to *truly* experience life as it was intended.

TO GO DEEPER THIS WEEK . . .
» Read Jeremiah 29:11.
» Read Matthew 28:18-20.
» Read John 10:10.

1. What are some ways you may cling to your life rather than dying to yourself?
2. What are some specific areas where you believe God intends for you to have an impact?

ACKNOWLEDGMENTS

I am so grateful to my Father in heaven and the Lord Jesus Christ for giving me loving parents, Tandy and Debbie Gerelds, and for allowing me to witness His work in their lives. Additionally, I am grateful to have seen His work in the lives of my sisters, Jill and Jessica, and in the countless lives of the people who were influenced by my dad through various seasons of life.

I am extremely grateful to and challenged by the team at Tyndale House, whose commitment to excellence and to glorifying God through their work is apparent to anyone with whom they work. I want to thank my editor, Sarah Rubio, who is amazing in her ability to corral me from rabbit trails and to keep the main thing, the main thing. Thanks to Jon Farrar for believing in this project and making it happen. Thank you to Sharon Leavitt for loving the Tyndale authors and praying for me and my family. Thanks to Ron Beers, Jan Long Harris, Cassidy Gage, Jillian Schlossberg, Kara Leonino, Deborah King, Cheryl

Warner, Donna Berg, Todd Starowitz, Emily Bonga, Andrea Martin, Dave Endrody, Sharon Heggeland, John Johnson, Mark DiCicco, Mike Morrison, Babette Rea, James Elwell, and Eric Siewert. You all are amazing, and your love for God and people shines through in the work you do. Thank you for being such a great team! You have made an impact on my life.

Thank you to Brian Mitchell at WTA Group for getting behind this project and getting it to the team at Tyndale. Thank you to my friend, brother, and partner in ministry, Chris Corder—I'm not sure how you've been able to do the things you've done for me. Thank you to Andy and Jon Erwin (*Woodlawn* producers) for giving me the opportunity to tell my dad's story to such a huge audience. Thanks to my work sister, Mary Beth, for working with a guy who may be going in a thousand different directions at one time.

Thank you to my daughters, Morgan, Bailey Kay (BK), Alli, and Maggie Leigh, for loving your flawed daddy and for the inspiration you give me every day. Finally, thank you to my writing mentor, best friend, wife, and very favorite person in the world, Jennifer Gerelds. Your ability to run our house, write, and take care of four daughters and me with grace and love is incomprehensible. Thank you for your encouragement to me in my writing and speaking, and for making it possible and pushing me to go get my writing done! I love you.

ABOUT THE AUTHOR

TODD GERELDS is author of the book *Woodlawn*, a dramatic, powerful, and true story of redemption and reconciliation that occurred in the middle of what many say was the most racially charged and volatile era of Birmingham, Alabama's history. The miraculous events that Todd witnessed as the young son of Coach Tandy Gerelds—Woodlawn High School's football coach in the early 1970s—became a major motion picture that played in thousands of theaters across the country. Its message of hope, faith, and God's incredible power to change lives through love has made a huge impact in public and private schools, churches, athletic teams, businesses, charity organizations, and many individual lives.

In his book, Todd recounts how he witnessed God's amazing love transform his dad, a team, a school, and even a city as he tagged along to practices and games with his father. Though the events unfolded decades ago, the message of grace, love, and change that is possible through Jesus has fresh relevance for today's culture. Many Christian leaders and pastors believe that God is using this amazingly timely story to do a major work among His people, this country, and even the world. Todd's talks are driven by the passion he feels about having personally experienced God's life-changing love and the extraordinary work he believes God accomplishes every day through ordinary people.

God has uniquely positioned and gifted Coach Gerelds's son to not only tell this story but also to truly equip and enhance other people's lives in the process. Through years of training under and playing football for Coach Gerelds, Todd inherited his dad's love and skill for coaching. Like his father, Todd loves to help individuals and groups recognize their gifts, capitalize on their strengths, and most importantly, learn how to relate and work well with others on their team to achieve a greater result. But Todd has not exercised his coaching skills on the football field. Instead, he has devoted them to the professional world, particularly in the diverse, innovative, and competitive medical field. Todd has spent more than twenty years in the medical device, pharmaceutical, and biotech industries, helping clinicians and their patients. Serving in diverse capacities as field rep and district manager, national sales trainer and personal counselor and mentor, Todd has poured his life into equipping patients, colleagues, doctors, and friends to live better lives. As a result, he has consistently ranked as a top performer, earning a wide variety of sales awards with three Fortune 500 companies.

Those who know Todd describe him as possessing an uncanny ability to draw even the most introverted stranger into lively and then deep-hearted conversation. His natural gift of relating and connecting with people of all walks of life has earned him strong recognition as an engaging, informative, and effective keynote speaker for churches, ministries, sports teams, businesses, and civic and charitable functions. He speaks on topics of leadership, integrity, and talent and character development in both the personal and professional realm.

Todd Gerelds is a dynamic speaker whose message of love, reconciliation, and identity in Christ has touched thousands of lives across the nation. With their broad appeal to people of different ages, races, and backgrounds, Todd's talks have had a profound impact on church groups, athletic teams and coaches, schools, civic groups, and more, inspiring and uniting individuals to recognize the unique role each one has to play in showing God's love and making this world a better place in the process.

For booking information go to
toddgerelds.com or
e-mail booking@toddgerelds.com.

CP1535